Uncovering Our Masks

A Freud Reader

Uncovering Our Masks

A Freud Reader

EDITED WITH COMMENTARY BY
Bruce P. Lapenson

TEMPLE UNIVERSITY PRESS

PHILADELPHIA

Temple University Press, Philadelphia 19122
Copyright © 2003 by Temple University
All rights reserved
Published 2003
Printed in the United States of America

♾ The paper used in this publication meets the requirements
of the American National Standard for Information Sciences—Permanence
of Paper for Printed Library Materials, ANSI Z39.48-1984

ISBN 1-59213-216-2

2 4 6 8 9 7 5 3 1

Contents

Introduction   vii

PART ONE
The Development of Psychoanalysis   1

An Autobiographical Study   3

Introductory Lectures on Psycho-Analysis   13

The Psychopathology of Everyday Life   35

An Outline of Psycho-Analysis   37

Three Essays on the Theory of Sexuality   39

Jokes and Their Relation to the Unconscious   55

The Ego and the Id   57

Some Psychical Consequences of the
Anatomical Distinction Between the Sexes   65

Notes upon a Case of Obsessional Neurosis   68

The Psychogenesis of a Case of Homosexuality
in a Woman   85

Female Sexuality   95

The Dissolution of the Oedipus Complex   101

PART TWO
Psychoanalytic Interpretations of Culture 103

Totem and Taboo 105

The Future of an Illusion 118

Group Psychology and the Analysis of the Ego 123

Civilization and Its Discontents 131

PART THREE
Master Passages: Freud's Observations on Psychoanalysis and Its Uses 139

Notes 145

Introduction

Sigmund Freud (1856–1939) was an Austrian physician who developed the theory and practice of psychoanalysis. Freudian terms and references are quite common in the daily lexicon and mass media, and many Americans recognize the name "Freud." According to Jared Diamond, a professor of physiology at UCLA: "Freud's status is unique because he recognized an entirely different mental realm, and many of his concepts—pioneering and radical in their time—are so familiar today that they have entered the daily vocabulary."[1] In one sense, the mass recognition of anyone is a dreadful thing; a name becomes associated with a few highly simplified notions, and the bulk of the thinker's work is disregarded or unknown. Freud is among those whose work has been tragically simplified. This reader intends to expand the common and narrow understanding of Freud and his work.

Why study Freud? At the least, Freud's bedrock belief that humans are essentially animals who are coerced by institutions (family, religion, law, community norms) into redirecting their aggressive and pleasure-seeking nature toward socially acceptable, civil activities asks for our attention since it is so unflattering! While we have studied the Enlightenment and have heard the strong case for humans as reasoning, social, and cooperative beings, the Freudian view startles us and muddies the whole picture. The complexity of Freudian theory emerges through its claims that there is a reason for the most apparently irrational of human actions. Freud knew that we are capable of being civil, humane, and creative in a positive way, but he also loudly proclaimed that the Enlightenment view of humans is a "one-sided ethical valuation."[2] Freudian theory may help us with the following enduring questions:

> As our scientific endeavours solve more puzzles about our bodies and the physical universe, why does our social life, not infrequently, remain riddled with aggression, prejudice, and oppression?
>
> Why have highly "civilized" cultures and religious institutions committed some of the greatest incivilities?

Why do some individuals continue self-destructive behavior while fully aware of
   the potential consequences?
Why do hate groups remain attractive to some people?

Answering these difficult questions involves delving into the psyche of individuals
and of humans as a species.

Part One of this reader explores the development of psychoanalysis; it ends with
two of Freud's cases that illuminate his theories and the techniques he used with his
patients. Part Two explores Freud's later work—psychoanalytic interpretations of culture. Part Three presents a collection of notable quotations from Freud's work.

Freud emphasized the complexity of the human mind. He recognized, as Jared Diamond pointed out, "that unique two-way relationship [of analyst and analysand]"[3]
and that the therapist–client struggle reflected the latter's difficulties outside the analyst's office. Depression, anxiety, panic, phobias, etc., are replacements for especially
troubling past events, usually involving significant others, that a person has repressed
and that she or he is not ready to confront. In this way, puzzling, destructive, self-destructive, irrational, or bizarre behavior follows a logic hidden in the troubled individual's memories. Excavation will be slow and acknowledgement even slower. Why
would the ego give up *what it has created to protect itself?*

Psychoanalytic theory focuses on the ambivalent feelings we tend to have for loved
ones, authority figures, and culture itself. Contradictory attitudes reveal themselves
in our popular culture. The movie *Fargo,* when shown on television recently, displayed
its share of human depravity, but the dialogue was censored each time a character
used profanity. It is difficult to find situation comedies on television without frequent
sexual innuendo and very sexually attractive characters, but the most "risqué" word
allowed is "ass." We can also think in Freudian ways about the political purposes of
cultural trends. The more outlets Americans have for emotional release from the long
work week, economic insecurity, and fears about crime and violence, the less likely are
significant numbers of citizens to express these frustrations and concerns in an organized political form.[4]

Where does Freudian thought leave our perpetual hopes for "peace on Earth" and
"goodwill to mankind"? We could say that such pursuits are a work in progress, and
then ask ourselves if our culture has become more civil during the past century. Is the
increase in sexual freedom of the past three decades a good or bad thing, or both?
Where would Freud come down on this question? The common perception of Freud
might be challenged here. What would result if portrayals of violence in our mass
media were eliminated or significantly decreased? Quite simply, as Freud asked, will
societies be successful in their attempts at balancing freedom and restrictions, or is this
problem irreconcilable?

Editor's Commentary and Questions

The editor's comments are indented to distinguish them from the excerpts from
Freud's work. Professors can use the questions from the editor's commentary as part

of lectures and discussions to provoke thinking and elicit responses from students regarding in-class or assigned readings. The questions are meant to assist students when they attempt to pinpoint what is central about an excerpt they are about to read but also to help them keep in mind what they previously read; that is, excerpts and commentary are placed in each work of Freud's to provide a sequence of points that lead to an overarching point or concept.

Part One

The Development
of Psychoanalysis

We will focus in Part One on the influences that led Sigmund Freud to develop psychoanalysis, a form of psychotherapy which engages the patient in an exploration of important, but forgotten past events that are assumed to be the cause of current difficulties in the patient's life. As we come to understand Freudian concepts, we will see how Freud used psychoanalytic techniques with two of his patients.

An Autobiographical Study

From 1876 to 1882, Freud worked in the laboratory of the renowned German physiologist Ernst von Brucke. In 1885 he was appointed lecturer in neuropathology at the University of Vienna, and soon after, thanks to a strong recommendation from Brucke, traveled to Paris and studied with Jean Martin Charcot.[1] Charcot discovered that paralysis and contractures (e.g., immobilization or impairments of the fingers, hands, or limbs) could be produced by a physician's suggestions to the subject. We know that paralysis can result from severe external and internal traumas to the body (car accidents, falls, blows, strokes). But how could mere words produce a paralyzed limb? During the trial of Nazi Adolf Eichmann, a concentration camp survivor suffered a paralytic stroke while testifying. Perhaps the human body is vulnerable to mental processes. Mental or physical disease may have non-organic causes.

What impressed me most of all while I was with Charcot were his latest investigations upon hysteria, some of which were carried out under my own eyes. He had proved, for instance, the genuineness of hysterical phenomena and their conformity to laws (*"introite et hic dii sunt"* ["Enter, for here too are gods"]), the frequent occurrence of hysteria in men, the production of hysterical paralyses and contractures by hypnotic suggestion and the fact that such artificial products showed, down to their smallest details, the same features as spontaneous attacks, which were often brought on traumatically. Many of Charcot's demonstrations began by provoking in me and in other visitors a sense of astonishment and an inclination to scepticism, which we tried to justify by an appeal to one of the theories of the day. He was always friendly and patient in dealing with such doubts, but he was also most decided; it was in one of these discussions that (speaking of theory) he remarked, *"Ça n'empêche pas d'exister,"*[2] a *mot* which left an indelible mark upon my mind.

The excerpts in this section are taken from pages 13–30 of *An Autobiographical Study* by Sigmund Freud, translated by James Strachey. Copyright 1952 by W. W. Norton & Company, Inc., renewed © 1980 by Alix Strachey. Copyright 1935 by Sigmund Freud, renewed © 1963 by James Strachey. Used by permission of W. W. Norton & Company, Inc.

No doubt not the whole of what Charcot taught us at that time holds good to-day: some of it has become doubtful, some has definitely failed to withstand the test of time. But enough is left over that has found a permanent place in the storehouse of science. Before leaving Paris I discussed with the great man a plan for a comparative study of hysterical and organic paralyses. I wished to establish the thesis that in hysteria paralyses and anaesthesias of the various parts of the body are demarcated according to the popular idea of their limits and not according to anatomical facts. He agreed with this view, but it was easy to see that in reality he took no special interest in penetrating more deeply into the psychology of the neuroses. When all is said and done, it was from pathological anatomy that his work had started.

> In the following passage, note the reaction of Freud's fellow Viennese physicians to Charcot's discoveries, and Freud's status among his peers even after he demonstrates evidence for Charcot.

I will now return to the year 1886, the time of my settling down in Vienna as a specialist in nervous diseases. The duty devolved upon me of giving a report before the "Gesellschaft der Aerzte" [Society of Medicine] upon what I had seen and learnt with Charcot. But I met with a bad reception. Persons of authority, such as the chairman (Bamberger, the physician), declared that what I said was incredible. Meynert challenged me to find some cases in Vienna similar to those which I had described and to present them before the Society. I tried to do so; but the senior physicians in whose departments I found any such cases refused to allow me to observe them or to work at them. One of them, an old surgeon, actually broke out with the exclamation: "But, my dear sir, how can you talk such nonsense? *Hysteron* [sic] means the uterus. So how can a man be hysterical?"[3] I objected in vain that what I wanted was not to have my diagnosis approved, but to have the case put at my disposal. At length, outside the hospital, I came upon a case of classical hysterical hemi-anaesthesia in a man, and demonstrated it before the "Gesellschaft der Aerzte" [1886]. This time I was applauded, but no further interest was taken in me. The *impression* that the high authorities had rejected my innovations remained unshaken; and, with my hysteria in men and my production of hysterical paralyses by suggestion, I found myself forced into the Opposition. As I was soon afterwards excluded from the laboratory of cerebral anatomy and for terms on end had nowhere to deliver my lectures, I withdrew from academic life and ceased to attend the learned societies. It is a whole generation since I have visited the "Gesellschaft der Aerzte."

> During the late 1880s, Freud decided to pursue the treatment of nervous disorders. At this time, hysterics and others suffering from such maladies had few effective treatment options. To Freud, hypnotism appeared the most promising treatment, and Freud's and Bernheim's experiments with hypnotism profoundly affected the course of intellectual history.

Anyone who wants to make a living from the treatment of nervous patients must clearly be able to do something to help them. My therapeutic arsenal contained only two weapons, electrotherapy and hypnotism, for prescribing a visit to a hydropathic establishment after a single consultation was an inadequate source of income. My knowledge of electrotherapy was derived from W. Erb's text-book [1882], which provided detailed instructions for the treatment of all the symptoms of nervous diseases. Unluckily I was soon driven to see that following these instructions was of no help whatever and that what I had taken for an epitome of exact observations was merely the construction of phantasy. The realization that the work of the greatest name in German neuropathology had no more relation to reality than some "Egyptian" dreambook, such as is sold in cheap book-shops, was painful, but it helped to rid me of another shred of the innocent faith in authority from which I was not yet free. So I put my electrical apparatus aside, even before Moebius had saved the situation by explaining that the successes of electric treatment in nervous disorders (in so far as there were any) were the effect of suggestion on the part of the physician.

With hypnotism the case was better. While I was still a student I had attended a public exhibition given by Hansen the "magnetist," and had noticed that one of the subjects experimented upon had become deathly pale at the onset of cataleptic rigidity and had remained so as long as that condition lasted. This firmly convinced me of the genuineness of the phenomena of hypnosis. Scientific support was soon afterwards given to this view by Heidenhain; but that did not restrain the professors of psychiatry from declaring for a long time to come that hypnotism was not only fraudulent but dangerous and from regarding hypnotists with contempt. In Paris I had seen hypnotism used freely as a method for producing symptoms in patients and then removing them again. And now the news reached us that a school had arisen at Nancy which made an extensive and remarkably successful use of suggestion, with or without hypnosis, for therapeutic purposes. It thus came about, as a matter of course, that in the first years of my activity as a physician my principal instrument of work, apart from haphazard and unsystematic psycho-therapeutic methods, was hypnotic suggestion.

This implied, of course, that I abandoned the treatment of organic nervous diseases; but that was of little importance. For on the one hand the prospects in the treatment of such disorders were in any case never promising, while, on the other hand, in the private practice of a physician working in a large town, the quantity of such patients was nothing compared to the crowds of neurotics, whose number seemed further multiplied by the way in which they hurried, with their troubles unsolved, from one physician to another. And, apart from this, there was something positively seductive in working with hypnotism. For the first time there was a sense of having overcome one's helplessness; and it was highly flattering to enjoy the reputation of being a miracle-worker. It was not until later that I was to discover the drawbacks of the procedure. At the moment there were only two points to complain of: first, that I could not succeed in hypnotizing every patient, and secondly, that I was unable to put individual patients into as deep a state of hypnosis as I should have wished. With the idea of perfecting my hypnotic technique, I made a journey to Nancy in the summer of 1889 and spent several weeks there. I witnessed the moving spectacle of old [Auguste] Liebeault working among the poor women and children of the labouring classes. I was a spectator of [Professor Hippolyte] Bernheim's astonishing experiments upon his hospital patients, and I received the profoundest impression of the possibility that there could be powerful mental processes which nevertheless remained hidden from the consciousness of men. Thinking it would be instructive, I had persuaded one of my patients to follow me to Nancy. This patient was a very highly gifted hysteric, a woman of good birth, who had been handed over to me because no one knew what to do with her. By hypnotic influence I had made it possible for her to lead a tolerable existence and I was always able to take her out of the misery of her condition. But she always relapsed again after a short time, and in my ignorance I attributed this to the fact that her hypnosis had never reached the stage of somnambulism with amnesia. Bernheim now attempted several times to bring this about, but he too failed. He frankly admitted to me that his great therapeutic successes by means of suggestion were only achieved in his hospital practice and not with his private patients.

> From Josef Breuer, Freud learned to question hysterics under hypnosis about their lives and symptoms. The elimination of symptoms through this method was impressive, but the gradual development of the concepts of repression and the unconscious mind were of greater significance. Picture a boy who is not allowed to react to his parents' frequent loud and angry arguments during his early years. However, on numerous occasions this boy wants very much to react; he has various thoughts and emotions he wants to express. Where does his energy (emotions, thoughts) go? We have all had thousands of experiences and thoughts in our lifetimes. How much of our experience do we consciously remember? Where are the rest of our experiences?

I must supplement what I have just said by explaining that from the very first I made use of hypnosis in *another* manner, apart from hypnotic suggestion. I used it for questioning the patient upon the origin of his symptom, which in his waking state he could often describe only very imperfectly or not at all. Not only did this method seem more effective than mere suggestive commands or prohibitions, but it also satisfied the curiosity of the physician, who, after all, had a right to learn something of the origin of the phenomenon which he was striving to remove by the monotonous procedure of suggestion.

The manner in which I arrived at this other procedure was as follows. While I was still working in Brucke's laboratory I had made the acquaintance of Dr. Josef Breuer, who was one of the most respected family physicians in Vienna, but who also had a scientific past, since he had produced several works of permanent value upon the physiology of respiration and upon the organ of equilibrium. He was a man of striking intelligence and fourteen years older than myself. Our relations soon became more intimate and he became my friend and helper in my difficult circumstances. We grew accustomed to share all our scientific interests with each other. In this relationship the gain was naturally mine. The development of psycho-analysis afterwards cost me his friendship. It was not easy for me to pay such a price, but I could not escape it.

Even before I went to Paris, Breuer had told me about a case of hysteria which, between 1880 and 1882, he had treated in a peculiar manner which had allowed him to penetrate deeply into the causation and significance of hysterical symptoms. This was at a time, therefore, when Janet's works still belonged to the future. He repeatedly read me pieces of the case history, and I had an impression that it accomplished more towards an understanding of neuroses than any previous observation. I determined to inform Charcot of these discoveries when I reached Paris, and I actually did so. But the great man showed no interest in my first outline of the subject, so that I never returned to it and allowed it to pass from my mind.

When I was back in Vienna I turned once more to Breuer's observation and made him tell me more about it. The patient[4] had been a young girl of unusual education and gifts, who had fallen ill while she was nursing her father, of whom she was devotedly fond. When Breuer took over her case it presented a variegated picture of paralyses with contractures, inhibitions and states of mental confusion. A chance observation showed her physician that she could be relieved of these clouded states of consciousness if she was induced to express in words the affective phantasy by which she was at the moment dominated. From this discovery Breuer arrived at a new method of treatment. He put her into deep hypnosis and made her tell him each time what it was that was oppressing her mind. After the attacks of depressive confusion had been overcome in this way, he employed the same procedure for removing her inhibitions and physical disorders. In her waking state the girl could no more describe than other patients how her symptoms had arisen, and she could discover no link between them and any experiences of her life. In hypnosis she immediately discovered the missing connection. It turned out that all her symptoms went back to moving events which she had experienced while nursing her father; that is to say, her symptoms had a meaning and were residues or reminiscences of those emotional situations. It was found in most instances that there had been some thought or impulse which she had had to suppress while she was by her father's sick-bed, and that, in place of it, as a substitute for it, the symptom had afterwards appeared. But as a rule the symptom was not the precipitate of a single such "traumatic" scene, but the result of a summation of a number of similar situations. When the patient recalled a situation of this kind in a hallucinatory way under hypnosis and carried through to its conclusion, with a free expression of emotion, the mental act which she had originally suppressed, the symptom was abolished and did not return. By this procedure Breuer succeeded, after long and painful efforts, in relieving his patient of all her symptoms.

The patient had recovered and had remained well and, in fact, had become capable of doing serious work. But over the final stage of this hypnotic treatment there rested a veil of obscurity, which Breuer never raised for me; and I could not understand why he had so long kept secret what seemed to me an invaluable discovery instead of making science the richer by it. The immediate question, however, was whether it was possible to generalize from what he had found in a single case. The state of things which he had discovered seemed to me to be of so fundamental a nature that I could not believe it could fail to be present in any case of hysteria if it had been proved to occur in a single one. But the question could only be decided by experience. I therefore began to repeat Breuer's investigations with my own patients and eventually, especially after my visit to Bernheim in 1889 had taught me the limitations of hypnotic suggestion, I worked at nothing else. After observing for several years that his findings were invariably confirmed in every case of hysteria that was accessible to such treatment, and after having accumulated a considerable amount of material in the shape of observations analogous to his, I proposed to him that we should issue a joint publication. At first he objected vehemently, but in the end he gave way, especially since, in the meantime, Janet's works had anticipated some of his results, such as the tracing back of hysterical symptoms to events in the patient's life, and their removal by means of hypnotic reproduction *in statu nascendi*. In 1893 we issued a preliminary communication, "On the Psychical Mechanism of Hysterical Phenomena," and in 1895 there followed our book, *Studies on Hysteria*.

If the account I have so far given has led the reader to expect that the *Studies on Hysteria* must, in all essentials of their material content, be the product of Breuer's mind, that is precisely what I myself have always maintained and what it has been my aim to repeat here. As regards the *theory* put forward in the book, I was partly responsible, but to an extent which it is to-day no longer possible to determine. That theory was in any case unpretentious and hardly went beyond the direct description of the observations. It did not seek to establish the nature of hysteria but merely to throw light upon the origin of its symptoms. Thus it laid stress upon the significance of the life of the emotions and upon the importance of distinguishing between mental acts which are unconscious and those which are conscious (or rather capable of being conscious); it introduced a dynamic factor, by supposing that a symptom arises through the damming-up of an affect and an economic factor, by regarding that same symptom as the product of the transformation of an amount of energy which would otherwise have been employed in some other way. (This latter process was described as *conversion*.) Breuer spoke of our method as *cathartic*; its therapeutic aim was explained as being to provide that the quota of affect used for maintaining the symptom, which had got on to the wrong lines and had, as it were, become strangulated there, should be directed on to the normal path along which it could obtain discharge (or *abreaction*). The practical results of the cathartic procedure were excellent. Its defects, which became evident later, were those of all forms of hypnotic treatment. . . . Its value as an abridged method of treatment was shown afresh by Simmel [1918] in his treatment of war neuroses in the German army during the Great War. The theory of catharsis had not much to say on the subject of sexuality. In the case histories which I contributed to the *Studies* sexual factors played a certain part, but scarcely more attention was paid to them than to other emotional excitations. Breuer wrote of the girl, who has since become famous as his first patient, that her sexual side was extraordinarily undeveloped. It would have been difficult to guess from the *Studies on Hysteria* what an importance sexuality has in the aetiology of the neuroses.

> Many of Freud's patients exhibited sexual dysfunction, and he began to explore early sexual[5] events as the possible origins of neurosis.

The theory which we had attempted to construct in the *Studies* remained, as I have said, very incomplete; and in particular we had scarcely touched on the problem of aetiology, on the question of the ground in which the pathogenic process takes root. I now learned from my rapidly increasing experience that it was not *any* kind of emotional excitation that was in action behind the phenomena of neurosis but habitually one of a sexual nature, whether it was a current sexual conflict or the effect of earlier sexual experiences. I was not prepared for this conclusion and my expectations played no part in it, for I had begun my investigation of neurotics quite unsuspectingly. While I was writing my "History of the Psycho-Analytic Movement" in 1914, there recurred to my mind some remarks that had been made to me by Breuer, Charcot, and Chrobak, which might have led me to this discovery earlier. But at the time I heard them I did not understand what these authorities meant; indeed they had told me more than they knew themselves or were prepared to defend. What I heard from them lay dormant and inactive within me, until the chance of my cathartic experiments brought it out as an apparently original discovery. Nor was I then aware that in deriving hysteria from sexuality I was going back to the very beginnings of medicine and following up a thought of Plato's. It was not until later that I learnt this from an essay by Havelock Ellis.

Under the influence of my surprising discovery, I now took a momentous step. I went beyond the domain of hysteria and began to investigate the sexual life of the so-called neurasthenics[6] who used to visit me in numbers during my consultation hours. This experiment cost me, it is true, my popularity as a doctor, but it brought me convictions which to-day, almost thirty years later, have lost none of their force. There was a great deal of equivocation and mystery-making to be overcome, but, once that had been done, it turned out that in all of these patients grave abuses of the sexual function were present. Considering how extremely widespread are these abuses on the one hand and neurasthenia on the other, a frequent coincidence between the two would not have proved much; but there was more in it than that one bald fact. Closer observation suggested to me that it was possible to pick out from the confused jumble of clinical pictures covered by the name of neurasthenia two fundamentally different types, which might appear in any degree of mixture but which were nevertheless to be observed in their pure forms. In the one type the central phenomenon was the anxiety attack with its equivalents, rudimentary forms and chronic substitutive symptoms; I consequently gave it the name of *anxiety neurosis*, and limited the term *neurasthenia* to the other type. Now it was easy to establish the fact that each of these types had a different abnormality of sexual life as its corresponding aetiological factor: in the former, *coitus interruptus*, unconsummated excitation and sexual abstinence, and in the latter, excessive masturbation and too numerous nocturnal emissions. In a few specially instructive cases, which had shown a surprising alteration in the clinical picture from one type to the other, it could be proved that there had been a corresponding change in the underlying sexual regime. If it was possible to put an end to the abuse and allow its place to be taken by normal sexual activity, a striking improvement in the condition was the reward.

As you recall, Breuer demurred when discussing the final stage of "Anna O.'s" treatment. Freud eventually realized that the patient had became delusional, believing herself to be carrying Breuer's child. If eliminating Anna's symptoms through hypnosis
resulted in a new one, then she was not cured. Freud's own experience with another
apparently successful patient led him to the idea of transference.[7] The use of hypnosis, which obscures the defenses[8] that are so essential to identify and work through
in therapy, was therefore abandoned by Freud. He replaced hypnosis with free association (talk) by the *conscious* patient.

During the years that followed the publication of the *Studies,* having reached these
conclusions upon the part played by sexuality in the aetiology of the neuroses, I read
some papers on the subject before various medical societies, but was only met with in-
credulity and contradiction. Breuer did what he could for some time longer to throw
the great weight of his personal influence into the scales in my favour, but he effected
nothing and it was easy to see that he too shrank from recognizing the sexual aetiology of the neuroses. He might have crushed me or at least disconcerted me by pointing to his own first patient, in whose case sexual factors had ostensibly played no part
whatever. But he never did so, and I could not understand why this was, until I came
to interpret the case correctly and to reconstruct, from some remarks which he had
made, the conclusion of his treatment of it. After the work of catharsis had seemed to
be completed, the girl had suddenly developed a condition of "transference love"; he
had not connected this with her illness, and had therefore retired in dismay. It was obviously painful to him to be reminded of this apparent *contretemps.* His attitude towards me oscillated for some time between appreciation and sharp criticism; then
accidental difficulties arose, as they never fail to do in a strained situation, and we
parted.

Another result of my taking up the study of nervous disorders in general was that
I altered the technique of catharsis. I abandoned hypnotism and sought to replace it
by some other method, because I was anxious not to be restricted to treating hysteri-
form conditions. Increasing experience had also given rise to two grave doubts in my
mind as to the use of hypnotism even as a means to catharsis. The first was that even
the most brilliant results were liable to be suddenly wiped away if my personal relation with the patient became disturbed. It was true that they would be re-established
if a reconciliation could be effected; but such an occurrence proved that the personal
emotional relation between doctor and patient was after all stronger than the whole
cathartic process, and it was precisely that factor which escaped every effort at control. And one day I had an experience which showed me in the crudest light what I
had long suspected. It related to one of my most acquiescent patients, with whom
hypnotism had enabled me to bring about the most marvelous results, and whom I
was engaged in relieving of her suffering by tracing back her attacks of pain to their
origins. As she woke up on one occasion, she threw her arms round my neck. The unexpected entrance of a servant relieved us from a painful discussion, but from that time
onwards there was a tacit understanding between us that the hypnotic treatment
should be discontinued. I was modest enough not to attribute the event to my own ir-

resistible personal attraction, and I felt that I had now grasped the nature of the mysterious element that was at work behind hypnotism. In order to exclude it, or at all events to isolate it, it was necessary to abandon hypnotism.

But hypnotism had been of immense help in the cathartic treatment, by widening the field of the patient's consciousness and putting within his reach knowledge which he did not possess in his waking life. It seemed no easy task to find a substitute for it. While I was in this perplexity there came to my help the recollection of an experiment which I had often witnessed while I was with Bernheim. When the subject awoke from the state of somnambulism, he seemed to have lost all memory of what had happened while he was in that state. But Bernheim maintained that the memory was present all the same; and if he insisted on the subject remembering, if he asseverated that the subject knew it all and had only to say it, and if at the same time he laid his hand on the subject's forehead, then the forgotten memories used in fact to return, hesitatingly at first, but eventually in a flood and with complete clarity. I determined that I would act in the same way. My patients, I reflected, must in fact "know" all the things which had hitherto only been made accessible to them in hypnosis; and assurances and encouragement on my part, assisted perhaps by the touch of my hand, would, I thought, have the power of forcing the forgotten facts and connections into consciousness. No doubt this seemed a more laborious process than putting the patients into hypnosis, but it might prove highly instructive. So I abandoned hypnotism, only retaining my practice of requiring the patient to lie upon a sofa while I sat behind him, seeing him, but not seen myself.

My expectations were fulfilled; I was set free from hypnotism. But along with the change in technique the work of catharsis took on a new complexion. Hypnosis had screened from view an interplay of forces which now came in sight and the understanding of which gave a solid foundation to my theory.

How had it come about that the patients had forgotten so many of the facts of their external and internal lives but could nevertheless recollect them if a particular technique was applied. Observation supplied an exhaustive answer to these questions. Everything that had been forgotten had in some way or other been distressing; it had been either alarming or painful or shameful by the *standards* of the subject's personality. It was impossible not to conclude that that was precisely why it had been forgotten—that is, why it had not remained conscious. In order to make it conscious again in spite of this, it was necessary to overcome something that fought against one in the patient; it was necessary to make efforts on one's own part so as to urge and compel him to remember. The amount of effort required of the physician varied in different cases; it increased in direct proportion to the difficulty of what had to be remembered. The expenditure of force on the part of the physician was evidently the measure of a *resistance* on the part of the patient. It was only necessary to translate into words what I myself had observed, and I was in possession of the theory of *repression*.

It was now easy to reconstruct the pathogenic process. Let us keep to a simple example, in which a particular impulsion had arisen in the subject's mind but was opposed by other powerful impulsions. We should have expected the mental conflict which now arose to take the following course. The two dynamic quantities—for our present purposes let us call them "the instinct" and "the resistance"—would struggle with each other for some time in the fullest light of consciousness, until the instinct was repudiated and the cathexis of energy withdrawn from its impulsion. This would have been the normal solution. In a neurosis, however (for reasons which were still unknown), the conflict found a different outcome. The ego drew back, as it were, on its first collision with the objectionable instinctual impulse; it debarred the impulse from access to consciousness and to direct motor discharge, but at the same time the impulse retained its full cathexis of energy. I named this process *repression*; it was a novelty, and nothing like it had ever before been recognized in mental life. It was obviously a primary mechanism of defence, comparable to an attempt at flight, and was only a forerunner of the later-developed normal condemning judgement. The first act of repression involved further consequences. In the first place the ego was obliged to protect itself against the constant threat of a renewed advance on the part of the repressed impulse by making a permanent expenditure of energy, an *anticathexis*, and it thus impoverished itself. On the other hand, the repressed impulse, which was now *unconscious*, was able to find means of discharge and of substitutive satisfaction by circuitous routes and thus to bring the whole purpose of the repression to nothing. In the case of conversion hysteria the circuitous route led to the somatic innervation; the repressed impulse broke its way through at some point or other and produced *symptoms*. The symptoms were thus results of a compromise, for although they were substitutive satisfactions they were nevertheless distorted and deflected from their aim owing to the resistance of the ego.

The theory of repression became the corner-stone of our understanding of the neuroses. A different view had now to be taken of the task of therapy. Its aim was no longer to "abreact" an affect which had got on to the wrong lines but to uncover repressions and replace them by acts of judgement which might result either in the accepting or in the condemning of what had formerly been repudiated. I showed my recognition of the new situation by no longer calling my method of investigation and treatment *catharsis* but *psycho-analysis*.

Introductory Lectures on Psycho-Analysis

The Interpretation of Dreams

Freud's treatment of his patients had evolved from the use of hypnosis to free association. He next sought other roads to a neurotic's unconscious; the most investigated was his or her dreams. The difficulty of dream interpretation lay in unlocking the personal meanings behind the dream's dense, bizarre, and seemingly nonsensical events. In the following passage, Freud mentions the conscious waking resistance of his patients to his interpretations of their dreams. However, this resistance to self-knowledge can be observed in the very nature of the dream-elements; if the dreamers *really wanted to know* why they exhibited their symptoms, the dream content would be clear and accessible.

Ladies and Gentlemen,— As you see, our study of parapraxes has not been unprofitable. Thanks to our labours over them we have, subject to the premises I have explained to you, achieved two things: a conception of the nature of dream-elements and a technique for interpreting dreams. The conception of dream-elements tells us that they are ungenuine things, substitutes for something else that is unknown to the dreamer (like the purpose of a parapraxis), substitutes for something the knowledge of which is present in the dreamer but which is inaccessible to him. We are in hopes that it will be possible to carry over the same conception to whole dreams, which are made up of such elements. Our technique lies in employing free association to these elements in order to bring about the emergence of other substitutive structures, which will enable us to arrive at what is concealed from view.

I now propose that we should introduce a change into our nomenclature which will give us more freedom of movement. Instead of speaking of "concealed," "inaccessible," or "ungenuine," let us adopt the correct description and say "inaccessible to the dreamer's consciousness" or "*unconscious*." I mean nothing else by this than what may be suggested to you when you think of a word that has escaped you or the disturbing purpose in a parapraxis—that is to say, I mean nothing else than "*unconscious at the moment*." In contrast to this, we can of course speak of the dream-elements themselves, and the substitutive ideas that have been newly arrived at from them by association, as "*conscious*." This nomenclature so far involves no theoretical construction. No objection can be made to using the word unconscious as an apt and easily understandable description.

If we carry over our conception of the separate elements to the whole dream, it follows that the dream as a whole is a distorted substitute for something else, something unconscious, and that the task of interpreting a dream is to discover this unconscious material. From this, however, there at once follow three important rules, which we must obey during the work of interpreting dreams.

(1) We must not concern ourselves with what the dream *appears* to tell us, whether it is intelligible or absurd, clear or confused, since it cannot possibly be the unconscious material we are in search of. (An obvious limitation to this rule will force itself on our notice later.) (2) We must restrict our work to calling up the substitutive ideas for each element, we must not reflect about them, or consider whether they contain anything relevant, and we must not trouble ourselves with how far they diverge from the dream-element. (3) We must wait till the concealed unconscious material we are in search of emerges of its own accord, exactly as the forgotten word "Monaco" did in the experiment I have described.

Now, too, we can understand to what extent it is a matter of indifference how much or how little the dream is remembered and, above all, how accurately or how uncertainly. For the remembered dream is not the genuine material but a distorted substitute for it, which should assist us, by calling up other substitutive images, to come nearer to the genuine material, to make what is unconscious in the dream conscious. If our memory has been inaccurate, therefore, it has merely made a further distortion of this substitute—a distortion, moreover, which cannot have been without a reason.

The work of interpreting can be performed on one's own dreams just as on other people's. In fact one learns more from one's own: the process carries more conviction. If, then, we make the attempt, we notice that something is opposing our work. It is true that ideas occur to us, but we do not allow all of them to count; testing and selecting influences make themselves felt. In the case of one idea we may say to ourselves: "No, this is not relevant, it does not belong here"; in the case of another: "this is too senseless" and of a third: "this is totally unimportant." And we can further observe how with objections of this sort we may smother ideas and finally expel them altogether, even before they have become quite clear. Thus on the one hand we keep too close to the idea which was our starting-point, the dream-element itself; and on the other hand we interfere with the outcome of the free associations by making a selection. If we are not by ourselves while interpreting the dream, if we get someone else to interpret it, we become very clearly aware of yet another motive which we employ in making this illicit selection, for sometimes we say to ourselves: "No, this idea is too disagreeable; I will not or cannot report it."

These objections are obviously a threat to the success of our work. We must guard against them, and in our own case we do so by firmly resolving not to give way to them. If we are analysing someone else's dream, we do so by laying it down as an inviolable rule that he must not hold back any idea from us, even if it gives rise to one of the four objections—of being too unimportant or too senseless or of being irrelevant or too distressing to be reported. The dreamer promises to obey the rule, and we may be annoyed afterwards to find how badly he keeps his promise when the occasion arises. We may explain this to ourselves to begin with by supposing that, in spite of our authoritative assurance, he has not yet realized the justification for free association, and, we may perhaps have the notion of first convincing him theoretically by giving him books to read or by sending him to lectures which may convert him into a supporter of our views on free association. But we shall be held back from blunders like this when we consider that in the case of ourselves, as to: the strength of whose convictions we can, after all, hardly be in doubt, the same objections arise to certain ideas and are only set aside subsequently—by a court of appeal, as it were.

Instead of being annoyed by the dreamer's disobedience, we may take advantage of these experiences by learning something new from them—something which is all the more important the less we are expecting it. We perceive that the work of interpreting dreams is carried out in the face of a *resistance,* which opposes it and of which the critical objections are manifestations. This resistance is independent of the dreamer's theoretical conviction. We learn still more, indeed. We discover that a critical objection of this kind never turns out to be justified. On the contrary the ideas which people try to suppress in this way turn out *invariably* to be the most important ones and those which are decisive in our search for the unconscious material. It amounts, in fact, to a special distinguishing mark, if an idea is accompanied by an objection like this.

This resistance is something entirely new: a phenomenon which we have come upon in connection with our premises, but one which was not included among them. The appearance of this new factor in our reckoning comes to us as a not altogether pleasant surprise. We suspect at once that it is not going to make our work any easier. It might mislead us into abandoning our whole concern with dreams: something so unimportant as a dream and, on top of that, all these difficulties instead of a simple straightforward technique! But, on the other hand, the difficulties might act precisely as a stimulus and make us suspect that the work will be worth the trouble. We regularly come up against resistance when we try to make our way forward from the substitute which is the dream-element to the unconscious material hidden behind it. So we may conclude that there must be something of importance concealed behind the substitute. Otherwise, what is the point of the difficulties that are trying to keep the concealment going? If a child refuses to open his clenched fist to show what he has in it, we may feel sure that it is something wrong—something he ought not to have.

The moment we introduce the dynamic idea of a resistance into the facts of the case, we must simultaneously reflect that this factor is something variable in quantity. There may be greater and smaller resistances, and we are prepared to find these differences showing themselves during our work as well. We may perhaps be able to link with this another experience we also meet with during the work of interpreting dreams: sometimes it requires only a single response, or no more than a few, to lead us from a dream-element to the unconscious material behind it, while on other occasions long chains of associations and the overcoming of many critical objections are required for bringing this about. We shall conclude that these differences relate to the changing magnitude of the resistance, and we shall probably turn out to be right. If the resistance is small, the substitute cannot be far distant from the unconscious material; but a greater resistance means that the unconscious material will be greatly distorted and that the path will be a long one from the substitute back to the unconscious material.

And now perhaps it is time to take a dream and try our technique upon it and see whether our expectations are confirmed. Yes, but what dream are we to choose for the purpose? You cannot imagine how hard I find it to decide; nor can I yet make the nature of my difficulties plain to you. There must obviously be dreams which have on the whole been subjected to only a little distortion and the best plan would be to begin with them. But what dreams have been least distorted? The ones that are intelligible and not confused, two examples of which I have already put before you? That would be leading us quite astray. Investigation shows that such dreams have been subjected to an extraordinarily high degree of distortion. If, however, I were to disregard particular requirements and were to select a dream at haphazard, you would probably be greatly disappointed. We might have to notice or record such a profusion of ideas in response to the separate dream-elements that we should be unable to make head or tail of the work. If we write down a dream and then make a note of all the ideas that emerge in response to it, these may prove to be many times longer than the text of the dream. The best plan would therefore seem to be choose out a number of short dreams for analysis, each of which will at least tell us something or confirm some point. So we will make up our minds to take that course, unless experience may perhaps show us where we can really find dreams that have been only slightly distorted.

I can however think of something else that will make things easier for us—something, moreover, which lies along our path. Instead of starting on the interpretation of *whole* dreams, we will restrict ourselves to a few dream-elements, and we will trace out in a number of examples how these can be explained by applying our technique to them.

(a) A lady reported that she very often dreamt when she was a child that *God wore a paper cocked-hat on his head.* What can you make of that without the dreamer's help?

It sounds completely nonsensical. But it ceases to be nonsense when we hear from the lady that she used to have a hat of that sort put on her head at meals when she was a child, because she could never resist taking furtive glances at her brothers' and sisters' plates to see whether they had been given larger helpings than she had. So the hat was intended to act like a pair of blinders. This, incidentally, was a piece of historical information and was given without any difficulty. The interpretation of this element and at the same time of the whole short dream was easily made with the help of a further idea that occurred to the dreamer: "As I had heard that God was omniscient and saw everything," she said, "the dream can only mean that I knew everything and saw everything, even though they tried to prevent me." Perhaps this example is too simple.

(b) A skeptical woman patient had a longish dream in the course of which some people told her about my book on jokes [1905] and praised it highly. Something came in then about a *"channel," perhaps it was another book that mentioned a channel, or something else about a channel . . . she didn't know . . . it was all so indistinct.*

No doubt you will be inclined to expect that the element "channel," since it was so indistinct, would be inaccessible to interpretation. You are right in suspecting a difficulty; but the difficulty did not arise from the indistinctness: both the difficulty and the indistinctness arose from another cause. Nothing occurred to the dreamer in connection with "channel," and *I* could of course throw no light on it. A little later—it was the next day, in point of fact—she told me that she had thought of something that *might* have something to do with it. It was a joke, too,—a joke she had heard. On the steamer between Dover and Calais a well-known author fell into conversation with an Englishman. The latter had occasion to quote the phrase: "Du sublime au ridicule il n'y a qu'un pas. [It is only a step from the sublime to the ridiculous.]" "Yes," replied the author, *"le Pas de Calais"*—meaning that he thought France sublime and England ridiculous. But the *Pas de Calais* is a channel—the English Channel. You will ask whether I think this had anything to do with the dream. Certainly I think so; and it provides the solution of the puzzling element of the dream. Can you doubt that this joke was already present before the dream occurred, as the unconscious thought behind the element "channel"? Can you suppose that it was introduced as a subsequent invention? The association betrayed the skepticism which lay concealed behind the patient's ostensible admiration; and her resistance against revealing this was no doubt the common cause both of her delay in producing the association and of the indistinctness of the dream-element concerned. Consider the relation of the dream-element to its unconscious background: it was, as it were, a fragment of the background, an allusion to it, but it was made quite incomprehensible by being isolated.

(c) As part of a longish dream a patient dreamt that *several members of his family were sitting round a table of a peculiar shape,* etc. It occurred to him in connection with the table that he had seen a piece of furniture of the kind when he was on a visit to a particular family. His thoughts then went on to say that there was a peculiar relationship between the father and son in this family; and he soon added that the same thing was true of the relationship between himself and his own father. So the table had been taken into the dream in order to point out this parallel.

This dreamer had been long familiar with the requirement of dream-interpretation. Another person might perhaps have taken objection to such a trivial detail as the shape of a table being made the subject of investigation. But in fact we regard nothing in a dream as accidental or indifferent, and we expect to obtain information precisely from the explanation of such trivial and pointless details. You may perhaps also feel surprised that the thought that "the same thing was true of us and of them" should have been expressed by, in particular, the choice of a table [*Tisch*]. But this too becomes clear when you learn that the name of the family in question was *Tischler* [literally, "carpenter"]. By making his relations sit at this *Tisch,* he was saying that they too were *Tischlers.* Incidentally, you will notice how inevitably one is led into being indiscreet when one reports these dream-interpretations. And you will guess that this is one of the difficulties I have hinted at over the choice of examples. I could easily have taken another example in place of this one, but I should probably merely have avoided this indiscretion at the price of committing another.

The moment seems to me to have arrived for introducing two terms, which we could have made use of long ago. We will describe what the dream actually tells us as the *manifest dream-content,* and the concealed material, which we hope to reach by pursuing the ideas that occur to the dreamer, as the *latent dream-thoughts.* Thus we are here considering the relations between the manifest content of the dream and the latent dream-thoughts as shown in these examples. These relations may be of very many different kinds. In examples *(a)* and *(b)* the manifest element is also a constituent of the latent thoughts, though only a small fragment of them. A small piece of the large and complicated psychical structure of unconscious dream-thoughts has made its way into the manifest dream as well—a fragment of them, or, in other cases, an allusion to them, a caption, as it were, or an abbreviation in telegraphic style. It is the business of the work of interpretation to complete these fragments or this allusion into a whole—which was achieved particularly nicely in the case of example *(b).* Thus one form of the distortion which constitutes the dream-work is replacement by a fragment or an allusion. In example *(c)* another kind of relation is to be observed in addition; and we shall find this expressed in a purer and clearer form in the examples which follow.

(d) The dreamer *was pulling a lady* (a particular one, of his acquaintance) *out from behind a bed.* He himself found the meaning of this dream-element from the first idea that occurred to him. It meant that he was giving this lady preference.

(e) Another man dreamt that *his brother was in a box [Kasten].* In his first response "*Kasten*" was, replaced by "*Schrank* [cupboard]," and the second gave the interpretation: his brother was restricting himself ["*schränkt sichein*"].

(f) The dreamer *climbed to the top of a mountain, which commanded an unusually extensive view.* This sounds quite rational and you might suppose that there is nothing to interpret in it and that all we have to do is to enquire what memory gave rise to the dream and the reason for its being stirred up. But you would be wrong. It turned out that this dream stood in need of interpreting just as much as any other, more confused one. For none of his own mountain climbs occurred to the dreamer, but he thought of the fact that an acquaintance of his was the editor of a "Survey," dealing with our relations with the *most remote* parts of the earth. Thus the latent dream-thought was an identification of the dreamer with the "surveyor."

Here we have a new type of relation between the manifest and latent dream-elements. The former is not so much a distortion of the latter as a representation of it, a plastic, concrete, portrayal of it, taking its start from the wording. But precisely on that account it is once more a distortion, for we have long since forgotten from what concrete image the word originated and consequently fail to recognize it when it is replaced by the image. When you consider that the manifest dream is made up predominantly of visual images and more rarely of thoughts and words, you can imagine what importance attaches to this kind of relation in the construction of dreams. You will see, too, that in this way it becomes possible in regard to a large number of abstract thoughts to create pictures to act as substitutes for them in the manifest dream while at the same time serving the purpose of concealment. This is the technique of the familiar *picture-puzzles*. Why it is that these representations have an appearance of being jokes is a special problem into which we need not enter here.

There is a fourth kind of relation between the manifest and latent elements, which I must continue to hold back from you until we come upon its key-word in considering technique. Even so I shall not have given you a full list; but it will serve our purpose.

Do you feel bold enough now to venture upon the interpretation of a *whole* dream? Let us make the experiment, to see whether we are well enough equipped for the task. I shall of course not select one of the most obscure ones; nevertheless, it will be one that gives a well-marked picture of the attributes of a dream.

> The dream presented below displays sparse manifest content, but the key to its latent meaning can be discerned when the dream is broken up into its various elements. Moreover, when helped by the dreamer supplying information, the dream reveals a unifying theme. As you will notice, detection of the theme is neither immediate nor obvious.

Very well then. A lady who, though she was still young, had been married for many years had the following dream: She was at the theatre with her husband. One side of the stalls was completely empty. Her husband told her that Elise L. and her fiancé had wanted to go too, but had only been able to get bad seats—three for 1 florin 50 kreuzers—and of course they could not take those. She thought it would not really have done any harm if they had.

The first thing the dreamer reported to us was that the precipitating cause of the dream was touched on in its manifest content. Her husband had in fact told her that Elise L., who was approximately her contemporary, had just become engaged. The dream was a reaction to this information We know already that it is easy in the case of many dreams to point to a precipitating cause like this from the previous day, and that the dreamer is often able to trace this for us without any difficulty. The dreamer in the present case put similar information at our disposal for other elements of the manifest dream as well.— Where did the detail come from about one side of the stalls being empty? It was an allusion to a real event of the previous week. She had planned to go to a particular play and had therefore bought her tickets *early*—so early that she had had to pay a booking fee. When they got to the theatre it turned out that her anxiety was quite uncalled-for, since *one side of the stalls was almost empty*. It would have been early enough if she had bought the tickets on the actual day of the performance. Her husband had kept on teasing her for having been in too much of a hurry.— What was the origin of the 1 florin 50 kreuzers? It arose in quite another connection, which had nothing to do with the former one but also alluded to some information from the previous day. Her sister-in-law had been given a present of 150 florins by her husband and had been in a great hurry—the silly goose—to rush off to the jewellers' and exchange the money for a piece of jewelry. Where did the "three" come from? She could think of nothing in connection with that, unless we counted the idea that her newly engaged friend, Elise L., was only three months her junior, though she herself had been a *married woman* for nearly ten years.— And the absurd notion of taking three tickets for only two people? She had nothing to say to that, and refused to report any further ideas or information.

But all the same, she had given us so much material in these few associations that it was possible to guess the latent dream-thoughts from them. We cannot help being struck by the fact that periods of time occur at several points in the information she gave us about the dream, and these provide a common factor between the different parts of the material. She took the theatre tickets *too early*, bought them *overhurriedly* so that she had to pay more than was necessary; so too her sister-in-law had been *in a hurry* to take her money to the jewellers and buy some jewelry with it, as though otherwise she would *miss it*. If, in addition to the "too early" and "in a hurry" which we have stressed, we take into account the precipitating cause of the dream—the news that her friend, though only three months *her junior,* had nevertheless got an excellent husband—and the criticism of her sister-in-law expressed in the idea that it was absurd of her to be in such a hurry, then we find ourselves presented almost spontaneously with the following construction of the latent dream-thoughts, for which the manifest dream is a severely distorted substitute:

"Really it was *absurd* of me to be in such a hurry to get married! I can see from Elise's example that *I* could have got a husband later too." (Being in too great a hurry was represented by her own behaviour in buying the tickets and by her sister-in-law's in buying the jewelry. Going to the play appeared as a substitute for getting married.) This would seem to be the main thought. We may perhaps proceed further, though with less certainty, since the analysis ought not to have been without the dreamer's comments at these points: "And I could have got one hundred times better with the money!" (150 florins is a hundred times more than 1 florin 50). If we were to put her dowry in place of the money, it would mean that her husband was bought with her dowry: the jewelry, and the bad tickets as well, would be substitutes for her husband. It would be still more satisfactory if the actual element "three tickets" had something to do with a husband. But we have not got so far as that in our understanding of the dream. We have only discovered that the dream expresses the *low value* assigned by her to her own husband and her regret at having *married so early.*

We shall, I fancy, be more surprised and confused than satisfied by the outcome of this first dream-interpretation. We have been given too much in one dose—more than we are yet able to cope with. We can already see that we shall not exhaust the lessons of this interpretation of a dream. Let us hasten to single out what we can recognize as established new discoveries.

In the first place, it is a remarkable thing that the main emphasis in the latent thoughts lies on the element of being in too great a hurry; nothing of the sort is to be found in the manifest dream. Without the analysis, we should have had no suspicion that that factor plays any part. It seems, therefore, to be possible for what is in fact the main thing, the centre of the unconscious thoughts, to be absent in the manifest dream. This means that the impression made by the whole dream must be fundamentally altered. In the second place, there is an absurd combination in the dream: three for 1 florin 50. We detected in the dream-thoughts the assertion that "it was absurd (to marry so early)." Can it be doubted that this thought, "it was absurd," is represented by the inclusion of an absurd element in the manifest dream? And in the third place, a glance of comparison shows us that the relation between the manifest and latent elements is no simple one; it is far from being the case that one manifest element always takes the place of one latent one. It is rather that there is a group-relation between the two layers, within which one manifest element can replace several latent ones or one latent element can be replaced by several manifest ones.

As regards the meaning of the dream and the dreamer's attitude to it, we might point out much that is similarly surprising. She agreed to the interpretation indeed, but she was astonished at it. She was not aware that she assigned such a low value to her husband; nor did she know *why* she should set such a low value on him. So there is still much that is unintelligible about it. It really seems to me that we are not yet equipped for interpreting a dream and that we need first to be given some further instruction and preparation.

> Having established the two categories of dream content, Freud explores the specific characteristic of censorship found in dreams. Notice how the dreamer, in waking life, has distanced herself from her product. Still, the manifest content suggests that, even while she dreams, she does not want to admit something to herself. A dream would therefore be strange, unexpected, or dense due to the dreamer's discomfort with her hidden wishes.

Ladies and Gentlemen,— The study of the dreams of children has taught us the origin, the essential nature and the function of dreams. *Dreams are things which get rid of (psychical) stimuli disturbing to sleep, by the method of hallucinatory satisfaction.* We have, however, only been able to explain one group of the dreams of adults—those which we have described as dreams of an infantile type. What the facts are about the others we cannot yet say, but we do not understand them. We have arrived at a provisional finding, however, whose importance we must not under-estimate. Whenever a dream has been completely intelligible to us, it has turned out to be the hallucinated fulfillment of a wish. This coincidence cannot be a chance one nor a matter of indifference.

We have assumed of dreams of another sort, on the basis of various considerations and on the analogy of our views on parapraxes, that they are a distorted substitute for an unknown content, and that the first thing is to trace them back to it. Our immediate task, then, is an enquiry which will lead to an understanding of this *distortion in dreams.*

Dream-distortion is what makes a dream seem strange and unintelligible to us. We want to know a number of things about it: firstly, where it comes from—its dynamics—, secondly, what it does and, lastly, how it does it. We can also say that dream-distortion is carried out by the dream-work; and we want to describe the dream-work and trace it back to the forces operating in it.

And now listen to this dream. It was recorded by a lady belonging to our group,[1] and, as she tells us, was derived from a highly esteemed and cultivated elderly lady. No analysis was made of the dream; our informant remarks that for a psycho-analyst it needs no interpreting. Nor did the dreamer herself interpret it, but she judged it and condemned it as though she understood how to interpret it; for she said of it: "And disgusting, stupid stuff like this was dreamt by a woman of fifty, who has no other thoughts day and night but worry about her child!"

Here then, is the dream—which deals with "love services" in war-time. "She went to Garrison Hospital No. I and informed the sentry at the gate that she must speak to the Chief Medical Officer (mentioning a name that was unknown to her) as she wanted to volunteer for service at the hospital. She pronounced the word 'service' in such a way that the NCO at once understood that she meant 'love service.' Since she was an elderly lady, after some hesitation he allowed her to pass. Instead of finding the Chief Medical Officer, however, she reached a large and gloomy apartment in which a number of officers and army doctors were standing and sitting round a long table. She approached a staff surgeon with her request, and he understood her meaning after she had said only a few words. The actual wording of her speech in the dream was: 'I and many other women and girls in Vienna are ready to . . .' at this point in the dream her words turned into a mumble '. . . for the troops—officers and other ranks without distinction.' She could tell from the expressions on the officers' faces, partly embarrassed and partly sly, that everyone had understood her meaning correctly. The lady went on: 'I'm aware that our decision must sound surprising, but we mean it in bitter earnest. No one asks a soldier in the field whether he wishes to die or not.' There followed an awkward silence of some minutes. The staff surgeon then put his arm round her waist and said: 'Suppose, madam, it actually came to . . . (mumble).' She drew away from him, thinking to herself: 'He's like all the rest of them,' and replied: 'Good gracious, I'm an old woman and I might never come to that. Besides, there's one condition that must be observed: age must be respected. It must never happen that an elderly woman . . . (mumble) . . . a mere boy. That would be terrible.' 'I understand perfectly,' replied the staff surgeon. Some of the officers, and among them one who had been a suitor of hers in her youth, laughed out loud. The lady then asked to be taken to the Chief Medical Officer, with whom she was acquainted, so that the whole matter could be thrashed out; but she found, to her consternation, that she could not recall his name. Nevertheless, the staff surgeon, most politely and respectfully, showed her the way up to the second floor by a very narrow, iron, spiral staircase, which led directly from the room to the upper storeys of the building. As she went up she heard an officer say: 'That's a tremendous decision to make—no matter whether a woman's young or old! Splendid of her!' Feeling simply that she was doing her duty, she walked up an interminable staircase."

The dream was repeated twice in the course of a few weeks, with, as the lady remarked, some quite unimportant and meaningless modifications.

From its continuous nature, the dream resembles a daytime phantasy: there are few breaks in it, and some of the details of its content could have been explained if they had been enquired into, but that, as you know, was not done. But what is remarkable and interesting from our point of view is that the dream shows several gaps—gaps not in the dreamer's memory of the dream but in the content of the dream itself. At three points the content was, as it were, extinguished; the speeches in which these gaps occurred were interrupted by a mumble. As no analysis was carried out, we have, strictly speaking, no right to say anything about the *sense* of the dream. Nevertheless there are hints on which conclusions can be based (for instance, in the phrase "love services"); but above all, the portions of the speeches immediately preceding the mumbles call for the gaps to be filled in, and in an unambiguous manner. If we make the insertions, the content of the phantasy turns out to be that the dreamer is prepared, by way of fulfilling a patriotic duty, to put herself at the disposal of the troops, both officers and other ranks, for the satisfaction of their erotic needs. This is, of course, highly objectionable, the model of a shameless libidinal phantasy—but it does not appear in the dream at all. Precisely at the points at which the context would call for this admission, the manifest dream contains an indistinct mumble: something has been lost or suppressed.

You will, I hope, think it plausible to suppose that it was precisely the objectionable nature of these passages that was the motive for their suppression. Where shall we find a parallel to such an event? You need not look far in these days. Take up any political newspaper and you will find that here and there the text is absent and in its place nothing except the white paper is to be seen. This, as you know, is the work of the press censorship. In these empty places there was something that displeased the higher censorship authorities and for that reason it was removed—a pity, you feel, since no doubt it was the most interesting thing in the paper—the "best bit."

On other occasions the censorship has not gone to work on a passage *after* it has already been completed. The author has seen in advance which passages might expect to give rise to objections from the censorship and has on that account toned them down in advance, modified them slightly, or has contented himself with approximations and allusions to what would genuinely have come from his pen. In that case there are no blank places in the paper, but circumlocutions and obscurities of expression appearing at certain points will enable you to guess where regard has been paid to the censorship in advance.

Well, we can keep close to this parallel. It is our view that the omitted pieces of the speeches in the dream which were concealed by a mumble have likewise been sacrificed to a censorship. We speak in so many words of a *"dream-censorship,"* to which some share in dream-distortion is to be attributed. Wherever there are gaps in the manifest dream the dream-censorship is responsible for them. We should go further, and regard it as a manifestation of the censorship wherever a dream-element is remembered especially faintly, indefinitely and doubtfully among other elements that are more clearly constructed. But it is only rarely that this censorship manifests itself so undisguisedly—so naively, one might say—as in this example of the dream of "love services." The censorship takes effect much more frequently according to the second method, by producing softenings, approximations and allusions instead of the genuine thing.

I know of no parallel in the operations of the press-censorship to a third manner of working by the dream-censorship; but I am able to demonstrate it from precisely the one example of a dream which we have analysed so far. You will recall the dream of the "three bad theatre-tickets for 1 florin 50." In the latent thoughts of that dream the element "over-hurriedly, too early" stood in the foreground. Thus: it was absurd to marry so *early*—it was also absurd to take the theatre-tickets so *early*—it was ridiculous of the sister-in-law to part with her money in such a *hurry* to buy jewelry with it. Nothing of this central element of the dream-thoughts passed over into the manifest dream; in it the central position is taken by the "going to the theatre" and "taking the tickets." As a result of this displacement of accent, this fresh grouping of the elements of the content, the manifest dream has become so unlike the latent dream-thoughts that no-one would suspect the presence of the latter behind the former. This displacement of accent is one of the chief instruments of dream-distortion and it is what gives the dream the strangeness on account of which the dreamer himself is not inclined to recognize it as his own production.

Omission, modification, fresh grouping of the material—these, then, are the activities of the dream-censorship and the instruments of dream-distortion. The dream-censorship itself is the originator, or one of the originators, of the dream-distortion which we are now engaged in examining. We are in the habit of combining the concepts of modification and re-arrangement under the term "displacement."

After these remarks on the activities of the dream-censorship, we will now turn to its dynamics. I hope you do not take the term too anthropomorphically, and do not picture the "censor of dreams" as a severe little manikin or a spirit living in a closet in the brain and there discharging his office; but I hope too that you do not take the term in too "localizing" a sense, and do not think of a "brain-centre," from which a censoring influence of this kind issues, an influence which would be brought to an end if the "centre" were damaged or removed. For the time being it is nothing more than a serviceable term for describing a dynamic relation. The word does not prevent our asking by what purposes this influence is exercised and against what purposes it is directed. And we shall not be surprised to learn that we have come up against the dream-censorship once already, though perhaps without recognizing it.

For that is in fact the case. You will recall that when we began to make use of our technique of free association we made a surprising discovery. We became aware that our efforts at proceeding from the dream-element to the unconscious element for which it is a substitute were being met by a *resistance*. This resistance, we said, could be of different magnitudes, sometimes enormous and sometimes quite insignificant. In the latter case we need to pass through only a small number of intermediate links in our work of interpretation; but when the resistance is large we have to traverse long chains of associations from the dream-element, we are led far away from it and on our path we have to overcome all the difficulties which represent themselves as critical objections to the ideas that occur. What we met with as resistance in our work of interpretation must now be introduced into the dream-work in the censorship. The resistance to interpretation is only a putting into effect of the dream-censorship. It also proves to us that the force of the censorship is not exhausted in bringing about the distortion of dreams and thereafter extinguished, but that the censorship persists as a permanent institution which has as its aim the maintenance of the distortion. Moreover, just as the strength of the resistance varies in the interpretation of each element in a dream, so too the magnitude of the distortion introduced by the censorship varies for each element in the same dream. If we compare the manifest and the latent dream, we shall find that some particular latent elements have been completely eliminated, others modified to a greater or less extent, while yet others have been carried over into the manifest content of the dream unaltered or even perhaps strengthened.

> The next section poses a question: If dream content often insults the dreamer's self-image and is so opposed to his or her waking beliefs, thoughts, and actions, why are such condemned contents not *infrequent* dream elements? To Freud, dream material hints at our origins and our true desires—freed from social norms and requirements, and legal and traditional coercions. The Enlightenment focused on our ability to reason about social and personal conflicts and therefore to achieve mutually advantageous resolutions. Freud praised our endurance, heroism, and accomplishments, while at the same time loudly proclaiming our capacity for the irrational. Absent our acknowledgement of such dark human capacities, their not infrequent demonstrations remain incomprehensible, and likely to return.

But we wanted to enquire what are the purposes which exercise the censorship and against what purposes it is directed. Now this question, which is, fundamental for the understanding of dreams and perhaps, indeed, of human life, is easy to answer if we look through the series of dreams which have been interpreted. The purposes which exercise the censorship are those which are acknowledged by the dreamer's waking judgement, those with which he feels himself at one. You may be sure that if you reject an interpretation of one of your own dreams which has been correctly carried out, you are doing so for the same motives for which the dream-censorship has been exercised, the dream-distortion brought about and the interpretation made necessary. Take the dream of our fifty-year-old lady. She thought her dream disgusting without having analysed it, and she would have been still more indignant if Dr. von Hug-Hellmuth had told her anything of its inevitable interpretation; it was precisely because of this condemnation by the dreamer that the objectionable passages in her dream were replaced by a mumble.

The purposes *against* which the dream-censorship is directed must be described in the first instance from the point of view of that agency itself. If so, one can only say that they are invariably of a reprehensible nature, repulsive from the ethical, aesthetic and social point of view—matters of which one does not venture to think at all, or thinks only with disgust. These wishes, which are censored and given a distorted expression in dreams, are first and foremost manifestations of an unbridled and ruthless egoism. And, to be sure, the dreamer's own ego appears in every dream and plays the chief part in it, even if it knows quite well how to hide itself so far as the manifest content goes. This *"sacro egoismo"*[2] of dreams is certainly not unrelated to the attitude we adopt when we sleep, which consists in our withdrawing our interest from the whole external world.

The ego, freed from all ethical bonds, also finds itself at one with all the demands of sexual desire, even those which have long been condemned by our aesthetic upbringing and those which contradict all the requirements of moral restraint. The desire for pleasure—the "libido," as we call it—chooses its objects without inhibition, and by preference, indeed, the forbidden ones: not only other men's wives, but above all incestuous objects, objects sanctified by the common agreement of mankind, a man's mother and sister, a woman's father and brother. (The dream of our fifty-year-old lady, too, was incestuous; her libido was unmistakably directed to her son. Lusts which we think of as remote from human nature show themselves strong enough to provoke dreams. Hatred, too, rages without restraint. Wishes for revenge and death directed against those who are nearest and dearest in waking life, against the dreamer's parents, brothers and sisters, husband or wife, and his own children are nothing unusual. These censored wishes appear to rise up out of a positive Hell; after they have been interpreted when we are awake, no censorship of them seems to us too severe.

But you must not blame the dream itself on account of its evil content. Do not forget that it performs the innocent and indeed useful function of preserving sleep from disturbance. This wickedness is not part of the essential nature of dreams. Indeed you know too that there are dreams which can be recognized as the satisfaction of justified wishes and of pressing bodily needs. These, it is true, have no dream-distortion; but they have no need of it, for they can fulfill their function without insulting the ethical and aesthetic purposes of the ego. Bear in mind, too, that dream-distortion is proportionate to two factors. On the one hand it becomes greater the worse the wish that has to be censored; but on the other hand it also becomes greater the more severe the demands of the censorship at the moment. Thus a strictly brought-up and prudish young girl, with a relentless censorship, will distort dream-impulses which we doctors, for instance, would have to regard as permissible, harmless, libidinal wishes, and on which in ten years' time the dreamer herself will make the same judgement.

Furthermore, we have not got nearly far enough yet to be able to feel indignant at this result of our work of interrelation. We do not yet, I think, understand it properly; but our first duty is to defend it against certain aspersions. There is no difficulty in finding a weak point in it. Our dream-interpretations are made on the basis of the premises which we have already accepted—that dreams in general have a sense, that it is legitimate to carry across from hypnotic to normal sleep the fact of the existence of mental processes which are at the time unconscious, and that everything that occurs to the mind is determined. If on the basis of these premises we had arrived at plausible findings from dream-interpretation, we should have been justified in concluding that the premises were valid. But how about it if these findings seem to be as I have pictured them? We should then be tempted to say: "These are impossible, senseless or at the least most improbable findings; so there was something wrong about the premises. Either dreams are not psychical phenomena, or there is nothing unconscious in the normal state, or our technique has a flaw in it. Is it not simpler and more satisfactory to suppose this rather than accept all the abominations which we are supposed to have discovered on the basis of our premises?"

Yes, indeed! Both simpler and more satisfactory—but not necessarily on that account more correct. Let us give ourselves time: the matter is not yet ripe for judgement. And first, we can further strengthen the criticism of our dream interpretations. The fact that the findings from them are so disagreeable and repellent need not, perhaps, carry very great weight. A stronger argument is that the dreamers to whom we are led to attribute such wishful purposes by the interpretation of their dreams reject them most emphatically and for good reasons. "What?" says one of them, "you want to convince me from this dream that I regret the money I have spent on my sister's dowry and my brother's education? But that cannot be so. I work entirely for my brothers and sisters; I have no other interest in life but to fulfill my duties to them, which, as the eldest of the family, I promised our departed mother I would do." Or a woman dreamer would say: "You think I wish my husband was dead? That is a shocking piece of nonsense! It is not only that we are most happily married—you would probably not believe me if I said that—but his death would rob me of everything I possess in the world." Or another man would answer us: "You say that I have sensual desires for my sister? That is ridiculous! She means nothing at all to me. We are on bad terms with each other and I have not exchanged a word with her for years." We might still take it lightly, perhaps, if these dreamers neither confirmed nor denied the purposes we attribute to them; we might say that these were just things they did not know about themselves. But when they feel in themselves the precise contrary of the wish we have interpreted to them and when they are able to prove to us by the lives they lead that they are dominated by this contrary wish, it must surely take us aback. Has not the time come to throw aside the whole work we have done on dream-interpretation as something which its findings have reduced *ad absurdum*?

No, not even now. Even this stronger argument collapses if we examine it critically. Granted that there are unconscious purposes in mental life, nothing is proved by showing that purposes opposed to these are dominant in conscious life. Perhaps there is room in the mind for contrary purposes, for contradictions, to exist side by side. Possibly, indeed, the dominance of one impulse is precisely a necessary condition of its contrary being unconscious. We are after all left, then, with the first objections that were raised: the findings of dream-interpretation are not simple and they are very disagreeable. We may reply to the first that all your passion for what is simple will not be able to solve a single one of the problems of dreams. You must get accustomed here to assuming a complicated state of affairs. And we may reply to the second that you are plainly wrong to use a liking or disliking that you may feel as the ground for a scientific judgement. What difference does it make if the findings of dream-interpretation seem disagreeable to you or, indeed, embarrassing and repulsive? "*Ça n'empêche pas d'exister,*"[3] as I heard my teacher Charcot say in a similar case when I was a young doctor. One must be humble and hold back one's sympathies and antipathies if one wants to discover what is real in this world. If a physicist were able to prove to you that in a short period organic life on this earth would be brought to an end by freezing, would you venture to make the same reply to him: "That cannot be so, the prospect is too disagreeable?" You would, I think, be silent, until another physicist came and pointed out to the first one an error in his premises or calculations. When you reject something that is disagreeable to you, what you are doing is *repeating* the mechanism of constructing dreams rather than understanding it and surmounting it.

You will promise now, perhaps, to disregard the repellent character of the censored dream-wishes and will withdraw upon the argument that after all it is unlikely that such a large space should be given to the evil in the constitution of human beings. But do your own experiences justify your saying this? I will not discuss how you may appear to yourselves; but have you found so much benevolence among your superiors and competitors, so much chivalry among your enemies and so little envy in your social surroundings that you feel it your duty to protest against egoistic evil having a share in human nature? Are you not aware of how uncontrolled and untrustworthy the average person is in everything to do with sexual life? Or do you not know that all the transgressions and excesses of which we dream at night are daily committed in real life by waking men? What does psycho-analysis do here but confirm Plato's old saying that the good are those who are content to dream of what the others, the bad, really do?

And now turn your eyes away from individuals and consider the Great War which is still laying Europe waste. Think of the vast amount of brutality, cruelty and lies which are able to spread over the civilized world. Do you really believe that a handful of ambitious and deluding men without conscience could have succeeded in unleashing all these evil spirits if their millions of followers did not share their guilt? Do you venture, in such circumstances, to break a lance on behalf of the exclusion of evil from the mental constitution of mankind?

You will represent to me that I am giving a one-sided judgement on the War: that it has also brought to light what is finest and noblest in men, their heroism, their self-sacrifice, their social sense. No doubt; but are you not now showing yourselves as accessories to the injustice that has so often been done to psycho-analysis in reproaching it with denying one thing because it has asserted another? It is not our intention to dispute the noble endeavours of human nature, nor have we ever done anything to detract from their value. On the contrary; I am exhibiting to you not only the evil dream-wishes which are censored but also the censorship, which suppresses them and makes them unrecognizable. We lay a stronger emphasis on what is evil in men only because other people disavow it and thereby make the human mind, not better, but incomprehensible. If now we give up this one-sided ethical valuation, we shall undoubtedly find a more correct formula for the relation between good and evil in human nature.

There it is, then. We need not give up the findings of our work on the interpretation of dreams even though we cannot but regard them as strange. Perhaps we shall be able to approach an understanding of them later from another direction. For the time being let us hold fast to this: dream-distortion is a result of the censorship which is exercised by recognized purposes of the ego against wishful impulses in any way objectionable that stir within us at night-time during our sleep. Why this should happen particularly at night-time and where these reprehensible wishes come from are matters on which, no doubt, much still remains for questioning and research.

> The dreams of different individuals share common objects and events, houses, water, snakes, departure. Freud deduced that these commonalties must be symbolic. Freud's developing belief that early sexual life (a term denoting all types of pleasure) was seminal to subsequent individual personality traits led him to view most dream symbols as sexual. Whether or not houses, trees, or vessels are permanent and universal sexual symbols, dream content, by standing for something other than its manifest presentations, again reveals the mind's ambivalence to self-discovery. Freud also calls our attention to the power of symbolism in our daily lives. We are struck by particular advertisements, movies, books, television shows, and political figures because they represent something significant to us. Not all symbols are sexual, but it is virtually impossible today to find a popular television show or movie without sexually appealing characters.

The range of things which are given symbolic representation in dreams is not wide: the human body as a whole, parents, children, brothers and sisters, birth, death, nakedness—and something else besides. The one typical—that is regular—representation of the human figure as a whole is a *house,* as was recognized by Scherner, who even wanted to give this symbol a transcendent importance which it does not possess. It may happen in a dream that one finds oneself climbing down the facade of a house, enjoying it at one moment, frightened at another. The houses with smooth walls are men, the ones with projections and balconies that one can hold on to are women.

One's parents appear in dreams as the Emperor and Empress, the *King* and *Queen* or other honoured personages; so here dreams are displaying much filial piety. They treat children and brothers and sisters less tenderly: these are symbolized as *small animals* or *vermin*. Birth is almost invariably represented by something which has a connection with *water*: one either falls into the water or climbs out of it, one rescues someone from the water or is rescued by someone—that is to say, the relation is one of mother to child. Dying is replaced in dreams by *departure*, by a *train journey*, being dead by various obscure and, as it were, timid hints, nakedness by *clothes* and *uniforms*. You see how indistinct the boundaries are here between symbolic and allusive representation.

It is a striking fact that, compared with this scanty enumeration, there is another field in which the objects and topics are represented with an extraordinarily rich symbolism. This field is that of sexual life—the genitals, sexual processes, sexual intercourse. The very great majority of symbols in dreams are sexual symbols. And here a strange disproportion is revealed. The topics I have mentioned are few, but the symbols for them are extremely numerous, so that each of these things can be expressed by numbers of almost equivalent symbols. The outcome, when they are interpreted, gives rise to general objection. For, in contrast to the multiplicity of the representations in the dream, the interpretations of the symbols are very monotonous, and this displeases everyone who hears of it; but what is there that we can do about it?

Since this is the first time I have spoken of the subject matter of sexual life in one of these lectures, I owe you some account of the way in which I propose to treat the topic. Psycho-analysis finds no occasion for concealments and hints, it does not think it necessary to be ashamed of dealing with this important material, it believes it is right and proper to call everything by its correct name, and it hopes that this will be the best way of keeping irrelevant thoughts of a disturbing kind at a distance. The fact that these lectures are being given before a mixed audience of both sexes can make no difference to this. Just as there can be no science *in usum Delphini*,[4] there can be none for school-girls; and the ladies among you have made it clear by their presence in this lecture-room that they wish to be treated on an equality with men.

The male genitals, then, are represented in dreams in a number of ways that must be called symbolic, where the common element in the comparison is mostly very obvious. To begin with, for the male genitals as a whole the sacred number 3 is of symbolic significance. The more striking and for both sexes the more interesting component of the genitals, the male organ, finds symbolic substitutes in the first instance in things that resemble it in shape-things, accordingly, that are long and up-standing, such as *sticks, umbrellas, posts, trees* and so on; further, in objects which share with the thing they represent the characteristic of penetrating into the body and injuring—thus, sharp weapons of every kind, *knives, daggers, spears, sabres*, but also fire-arms, *rifles, pistols* and *revolvers* (particularly suitable owing to their shape). In the anxiety dreams of girls, being followed by a man with a knife or a fire-arm plays a large part. This is perhaps the commonest instance of dream-symbolism and you will now be able to translate it easily. Nor is there any difficulty in understanding how it is that the male organ can be replaced by objects from which water flows—*water-taps, watering-cans,* or *fountains*—or again: by other objects which are capable of being lengthened, such as *hanging-lamps, extensible pencils,* etc. A no less obvious aspect of the organ explains the fact that *pencils, pen-holders, nail-files, hammers,* and other *instruments* are undoubted male sexual symbols.

The remarkable characteristic of the male organ which enables it to rise up in defiance of the laws of gravity, one of the phenomena of erection, leads to its being represented symbolically by *balloons, flying-machines* and most recently by *Zeppelin airships.* But dreams can symbolize erection in yet another, far more expressive manner. They can treat the sexual organ as the essence of the dreamer's whole person and make himself *fly.* Do not take it to heart if dreams of flying, so familiar and often so delightful, have to be interpreted as dreams of general sexual excitement, as erection-dreams. Among students of psycho-analysis, Paul Federn [1914] has placed this interpretation beyond any doubt; but the same conclusion was reached from his investigations by Mourly Vold [1910–12, 2, 791], who has been so much praised for his sobriety, who carried out the dream-experiments I have referred to with artificially arranged positions of the arms and legs and who was far removed from psychoanalysis and may have known nothing about it. And do not make an objection out of the fact that women can have the same flying dreams as men. Remember, rather, that our dreams aim at being the fulfilments of wishes and that the wish to be a man is found so frequently, consciously or unconsciously, in women. Nor will anyone with a knowledge of anatomy be bewildered by the fact that it is possible for women to realize this wish through the same sensations as men. Women possess as part of their genitals a small organ similar to the male one; and this small organ, the clitoris, actually plays the same part in childhood and during the years before sexual intercourse as the large organ in men.

Among the less easily understandable male sexual symbols are certain *reptiles* and *fishes,* and above all the famous symbol of the *snake.* It is certainly not easy to guess why *hats* and *overcoats* or *cloaks* are employed in the same way, but their symbolic significance is quite unquestionable. And finally we can ask ourselves whether the replacement of the male limb by another limb, the foot or the hand, should be described as symbolic. We are, I think, compelled to do so by the context and by counterparts in the case of women.

The female genitals are symbolically represented by all such objects as share their characteristic of enclosing a hollow space which can take something into itself: by *pits, cavities* and *hollows,* for instance, by *vessels* and *bottles,* by *receptacles, boxes, trunks, cases, chests, pockets,* and so on. Ships, too, fall into this category. Some symbols have more connection with the uterus than with the female genitals: thus, *cupboards, stoves* and, more especially, *rooms.* Here room-symbolism touches on house-symbolism. *Doors* and *gates,* again, are symbols of the genital orifice. Materials, too, are symbols for women: *wood, paper* and objects made of them, like *tables* and *books.* Among animals, *snails* and *mussels* at least are undeniably female symbols; among parts of the body, the *mouth* (as a substitute for the genital orifice); among buildings, *churches* and *chapels*. Not every symbol, as you will observe, is equally intelligible.

The breasts must be reckoned with the genitals and these, like the larger hemispheres of the female body, are represented by *apples, peaches,* and *fruit* in general. The pubic hair of both sexes is depicted in dreams as *woods* and *bushes*. The complicated topography of the female genital parts makes one understand how it is that they are often represented as *landscapes,* with rocks, woods and water, while the imposing mechanism of the male sexual apparatus explains why all kinds of complicated machinery which is hard to describe serve as symbols for it.

Another symbol of the female genitals which deserves mention is a *jewel-case. Jewel* and *treasure* are used in dreams as well as in waking life to describe someone who is loved. *Sweets* frequently represent sexual enjoyment. Satisfaction obtained from a person's own genitals is indicated by all kinds of *playing,* including *piano-playing.* Symbolic representations *par excellence* of masturbation are *gliding* or *sliding* and *pulling off a branch*. The *falling out of a tooth* or the *pulling out of a tooth* is a particularly notable dream-symbol. Its first meaning is undoubtedly castration as a punishment for masturbating. We come across special representations of sexual intercourse less often than might be expected from what has been said so far. Rhythmical activities such as *dancing, riding* and *climbing* must be mentioned here, as well as violent experiences such as *being run over;* so, too, certain *manual crafts,* and, of course, *threatening with weapons*.

You must not picture the use or the translation of these symbols as something quite simple. In the course of them all kinds of things happen which are contrary to our expectations. It seems almost incredible, for instance, that in these symbolic representations the differences between the sexes are often not clearly observed. Some symbols signify genitals in general, irrespective of whether they are male or female: for instance, a *small* child, a *small* son or a *small* daughter. Or again, a predominantly male symbol may be used for the female genitals or vice versa. We cannot understand this till we have obtained some insight into the development of sexual ideas in human beings. In some instances the ambiguity of the symbols may only be an apparent one; and the most marked symbols, such as *weapons, pockets* and *chests* are excluded from this bisexual use.

I will now go on to make a survey, starting not from the thing represented but from the symbol, of the fields from which sexual symbols are mostly derived, and I will make a few additional remarks, with special reference to the symbols where the common element in the comparison is not understood. The *hat* is an obscure symbol of this kind—perhaps, too, head-coverings in general—with a male significance as a rule, but also capable of a female one. In the same way an *overcoat* or *cloak* means a man, perhaps not always with a genital reference; it is open to you to ask why. Neckties, which hang down and are not worn by women, are a definitely male symbol. *Underclothing* and *linen* in general are female. *Clothes* and *uniforms,* as we have already seen, are a substitute for nakedness or bodily shapes. *Shoes* and *slippers* are female genitals. *Tables* and *wood* have already been mentioned as puzzling but certainly female symbols. *Ladders, steps* and *staircases,* or, more precisely, walking on them, are clear symbols of sexual intercourse. On reflection, it will occur to us that the common element here is the rhythm of walking up them—perhaps, too, the increasing excitement and breathlessness the higher one climbs.

We have earlier referred to *landscapes* as representing the female genitals. *Hills* and *rocks* are symbols of the male organ. *Gardens* are common symbols of the female genitals. *Fruit* stands, not for children, but for the breasts. *Wild animals* mean people in an excited sensual state, and further, evil instincts or passions. *Blossoms* and *flowers* indicate women's genitals, or, in particular, virginity. Do not forget that blossoms are actually the genitals of plants.

We are acquainted already with *rooms* as a symbol. The representation can be carried further, for windows, and doors in and out of rooms, take over the meaning of orifices in the body. And the question of the room being *open* or *locked* fits in with this symbolism, and the *key* that opens it is a decidedly male symbol. . . .

In the first place we are faced by the fact that the dreamer has a symbolic mode of expression at his disposal which he does not know in waking life and does not recognize. This is as extraordinary as if you were to discover that your housemaid understood Sanskrit, though you know that she was born in a Bohemian village and never learnt it. It is not easy to account for this fact by the help of our psychological views. We can only say that the knowledge of symbolism is unconscious to the dreamer, that it belongs to his unconscious mental life. But even with this assumption we do not meet the point. Hitherto it has only been necessary for us to assume the existence of unconscious endeavours, that is, of which, temporarily or permanently, we know nothing. Now, however, it is a question of more than this, of unconscious pieces of knowledge, of connections of thought, of comparisons between different objects which result in its being possible for one of them to be regularly put in place of the other. These comparisons are not freshly made on each occasion; they lie ready to hand and are complete, once and for all. This is implied by the fact of their agreeing in the case of different individuals—possibly, indeed, agreeing in spite of differences of language. What can be the origin of these symbolic relations? Linguistic usage covers only a small part of them. The multiplicity of parallels in other spheres of knowledge are mostly unknown to the dreamer; we ourselves have been obliged to collect them laboriously.

Secondly, these symbolic relations are not something peculiar to dreamers or to the dreamwork through which they come to expression. This same symbolism, as we have seen, is employed by myths and fairy tales, by the people in their sayings and songs, by colloquial linguistic usage and by the poetic imagination. The field of symbolism is immensely wide, and dream-symbolism is only a small part of it: indeed, it serves no useful purpose to attack the whole problem from the direction of dreams. Many symbols which are commonly used elsewhere appear in dreams very seldom or not at all. Some dream-symbols are not to be found in all other fields but only, as you have seen, here and there. One gets an impression that what we are faced with here is an ancient but extinct mode of expression, of which different pieces have survived in different fields, one piece only here, another only there, a third, perhaps, in slightly modified forms in several fields. And here I recall the phantasy of an interesting psychotic patient, who imagined a "basic language" of which all these symbolic relations would be residues.

Thirdly, it must strike you that the symbolism in the other fields I have mentioned is by no means solely sexual symbolism, whereas in dreams symbols are used almost exclusively for the expression of sexual objects and relations. This is not easily explained either. Are we to suppose that symbols which originally had a sexual significance later acquired another application and that, furthermore, the toning-down of representation by symbols into other kinds of representation may be connected with this? These questions can evidently not be answered so long as we have considered dream-symbolism alone. We can only hold firmly to the suspicion that there is a specially intimate relation between true symbols and sexuality.

The Psychopathology of Everyday Life

One may believe that speech mistakes and erroneous actions are produced by distractions, or are random events. But if the human mind has multiple layers—some more accessible than others—then perhaps some mistakes and errors have a purpose. Consider the examples of speech mistakes and other types of errors that Freud discusses in the following excerpt.

A . . . mechanism is shown in the mistake of another patient whose memory deserted her in the midst of a long-forgotten childish reminiscence. Her memory failed to inform her on what part of the body the prying and lustful hand of another had touched her. Soon thereafter she visited one of her friends, with whom she discussed summer homes. Asked where her cottage in M. was located, she answered, "Near the mountain loin" instead of "mountain lane."

Before calling on me, a patient telephoned for an appointment and also wished to be informed about my consultation fee. He was told that the first consultation was ten dollars; after the examination was over, he again asked what he was to pay and added: "I don't like to owe money to anyone, especially to doctors; I prefer to pay right away." Instead of *pay* he said *play*. His last voluntary remarks and his mistake put me on my guard, but after a few more uncalled-for remarks, he set me at ease by taking money from his pocket. He counted four paper dollars and was very chagrined and surprised because he had no more money with him and promised to send me a cheque for the balance. I was sure that his mistake betrayed him, that he was only *playing* with me, but there was nothing to be done. At the end of a few weeks, I sent him a bill for the balance, and the letter was returned to me by the post office authorities marked "Not found."

At a certain time twice a day for six years, I was accustomed to wait for admission before a door in the second story of the same house, and during this long period of time, it happened twice (within a short interval) that I climbed a story higher. On the first of these occasions, I was in an ambitious day-dream, which allowed me to "mount always higher and higher." In fact, at that time, I heard the door in question open as I put my foot on the first step of the third flight. On the other occasion, I again went too far, "engrossed in thought." As soon as I became aware of it, I turned back and sought to snatch the dominating phantasy; I found that I was irritated over a criticism of my works, in which the reproach was made that I "always went too far," which I replaced by the less respectful expression, "climbed too high."

An Outline of Psycho-Analysis

The Development of the Sexual Function

Prior to Freudian theory, the term *sexual life* had a narrow meaning. Struck by the frequency of deviations from "normal" sexual behavior and by the sexual interests of children, Freud broadened the meaning of the term.

According to the prevailing view human sexual life consists essentially in an endeavour to bring one's own genitals into contact with those of someone of the opposite sex. With this are associated, as accessory phenomena and introductory acts, kissing this extraneous body, looking at it and touching it. This endeavour is supposed to make its appearance at puberty—that is, at the age of sexual maturity—and to serve the purposes of reproduction. Nevertheless, certain facts have always been known which do not fit into the narrow framework of this view. (1) It is a remarkable fact that there are people who are only attracted by individuals of their own sex and by their genitals. (2) It is equally remarkable that there are people whose desires behave exactly like sexual ones but who at the same time entirely disregard the sexual organs or their normal use; people of this kind are known as "perverts." (3) And lastly it is a striking thing that some children (who are on that account regarded as degenerate) take a very early interest in their genitals and show signs of excitation in them.

It may well be believed that psycho-analysis provoked astonishment and denials when, partly on the basis of these three neglected facts, it contradicted all the popular opinions on sexuality. Its principal findings are as follows:

(a) Sexual life does not begin only at puberty, but starts with plain manifestations soon after birth.

(b) It is necessary to distinguish sharply between the concepts of "sexual" and "genital." The former is the wider concept and includes many activities that have nothing to do with the genitals.

(c) Sexual life includes the function of obtaining pleasure from zones of the body—a function which is subsequently brought into the service of reproduction. The two functions often fail to coincide completely.

The chief interest is naturally focused on the first of these assertions, the most unexpected of all. It has been found that in early childhood there are signs of bodily activity to which only an ancient prejudice could deny the name of sexual and which are linked to psychical phenomena that we come across later in adult erotic life—such as fixation to particular objects, jealousy, and so on. It is further found, however, that these phenomena which emerge in early childhood form part of an ordered course of development, that they pass through a regular process of increase reaching a climax towards the end of the fifth year, after which there follows a lull. During this lull progress is at a standstill and much is unlearnt and there is much recession. After the end of this period of latency, as it is called, sexual life advances once more with puberty; we might say that it has a second efflorescence. And here we come upon the fact that the onset of sexual life is *diphasic,* that it occurs in two waves—something that is unknown except in man and evidently has an important bearing on hominization.[1] It is not a matter of indifference that the events of this early period, except for a few residues, fall a victim to *infantile amnesia.* Our views on the aetiology of the neuroses and our technique of analytic therapy are derived from these conceptions and our tracing of the developmental processes in this early period has also provided evidence for yet other conclusions.

Three Essays on the Theory of Sexuality

The three essays that make up Freud's volume on the theory of sexuality are "The Sexual Aberrations," "Infantile Sexuality," and "The Transformations of Puberty." Excerpts from each essay follow.

From The Sexual Aberrations

Freud's early practice as a physician specializing in nervous disorders exposed him to the frequency of deviations from "normal" sexual behavior and provided new terrain for exploring the human mind. It was striking to Freud that strong cultural and moral restrictions regarding sexual expression were ignored by many of his neurotic patients. There must exist, he surmised, a link between neurosis and sexual life. Why would inanimate objects, children, or animals become a person's major or only sexual aim? Are such deviants merely "immoralists" by choice? Freud began to think that "perversions" had a beginning, and some series of early events had come to *dominate* the mind of the "pervert."

People whose sexual objects belong to the normally inappropriate sex—that is, inverts—strike the observer as a collection of individuals who may be quite sound in other respects. On the other hand, cases in which sexually immature persons (children) are chosen as sexual objects are instantly judged as sporadic aberrations. It is only exceptionally that children are the exclusive sexual objects in such a case. They usually come to play that part when someone who is cowardly or has become impotent adopts them as a substitute, or when an urgent instinct (one which will not allow of postponement) cannot at the moment get possession of any more appropriate object. Nevertheless, a light is thrown on the nature of the sexual instinct by the fact that it per-

The excerpts in this section are taken from Sigmund Freud's *Three Essays on the Theory of Sexuality*, edited and translated by James Strachey, in *Standard Edition of the Complete Psychological Works of Sigmund Freud*, Vol. 7 (London: Hogarth Press and Institute of Psycho-Analysis, 1953), pp. 148–229, by arrangement with Paterson Marsh Ltd., London.

mits of so much variation in its objects and such a cheapening of them—which hunger, with its far more energetic retention of its objects, would only permit in the most extreme instances. A similar consideration applies to sexual intercourse with animals, which is by no means rare, especially among country people, and in which sexual attraction seems to override the barriers of species.

One would be glad on aesthetic grounds to be able to ascribe these and other severe aberrations of the sexual instinct to insanity; but that cannot be done. Experience shows that disturbances of the sexual instinct among the insane do not differ from those that occur among the healthy and in whole races or occupations. Thus the sexual abuse of children is found with uncanny frequency among school teachers and child attendants, simply because they have the best opportunity for it. The insane merely exhibit any such aberration to an intensified degree; or, what is particularly significant, it may become exclusive and replace no sexual satisfaction entirely.

The very remarkable relation which thus holds between sexual variations and the descending scale from health to insanity gives us plenty of material for thought. I am inclined to believe that it may be explained by the fact that the impulses of sexual life are among those which, even normally, are the least controlled by the higher activities of the mind. In my experience anyone who is in any way, whether socially or ethically, abnormal mentally is invariably abnormal also in his sexual life. But many people are abnormal in their sexual life who in every other respect approximate to the average, and have, along with the rest, passed through the process of human cultural development, in which sexuality remains the weak spot.

UNSUITABLE SUBSTITUTES FOR THE SEXUAL OBJECT—FETISHISM

There are some cases which are quite specially remarkable—those in which the normal sexual object is replaced by another which bears some relation to it, but is entirely unsuited to serve the normal sexual aim. From the point of view of classification, we should no doubt have done better to have mentioned this highly interesting group of aberrations of the sexual instinct among the deviations in respect of the sexual *object*. But we have postponed their mention till we could become acquainted with the factor of sexual overvaluation, on which these phenomena, being connected with an abandonment of the sexual aim, are dependent.

What is substituted for the sexual object is some part of the body (such as the foot or hair) which is in general very inappropriate for sexual purposes, or some inanimate object which bears an assignable relation to the person whom it replaces and preferably to that person's sexuality (e.g. a piece of clothing or underlinen). Such substitutes are with some justice likened to the fetishes in which savages believe that their gods are embodied.

A transition to those cases of fetishism in which the sexual aim, whether normal or perverse, is entirely abandoned is afforded by other cases in which the sexual object is required to fulfil a fetishistic condition—such as the possession of some particular hair-colouring or clothing, or even some bodily defect—if the sexual aim is to be attained. No other variation of the sexual instinct that borders on the pathological can lay so much claim to our interest as this one, such is the peculiarity of the phenomena to which it gives rise. Some degree of diminution in the urge towards the normal sexual aim (an executive weakness of the sexual apparatus) seems to be a necessary precondition in every case.[1] The point of contact with the normal is provided by the psychologically essential overvaluation of the sexual object, which inevitably extends to everything that is associated with it. A certain degree of fetishism is thus habitually present in normal love, especially in those stages of it in which the normal sexual aim seems unattainable or its fulfillment prevented. . . .

The situation only becomes pathological when the longing for the fetish passes beyond the point of being merely a necessary condition attached to the sexual object and actually *takes the place* of the normal aim, and, further, when the fetish becomes detached from a particular individual and becomes the *sole* sexual object. These are, indeed, the general conditions under which mere variations of the sexual instinct pass over into pathological aberrations.

From Infantile Sexuality

Freud's exploration of the origins of neurosis begins at the inception of our lives. However, we do not remember much of our early life. Still, our minds might be most impressionable at this time, and more easily influenced by very early events because there has been much less time for the ego (person) to develop strength and defenses. Have most early events vanished, since we can recall so few of them? Does the lack of conscious memories render our early lives emotionally and psychologically insignificant?

NEGLECT OF THE INFANTILE FACTOR

One feature of the popular view of the sexual instinct is that it is absent in childhood and only awakens in the period of life described as puberty. This, however, is not merely a simple error but one that has had grave consequences, for it is mainly to this idea that we owe our present ignorance of the fundamental conditions of sexual life. A thorough study of the sexual manifestations of childhood would probably reveal the essential characters of the sexual instinct and would show us the course of its development and the way in which it is put together from various sources. It is noticeable that writers who concern themselves with explaining the characteristics and reactions of the adult have devoted much more attention to the primaeval period which is comprised in the life of the individual's ancestors—have, that is, ascribed much more influence to heredity—than to the other primaeval period, which falls within the lifetime of the individual himself—that is, to childhood. One would surely have supposed that the influence of this latter period would be easier to understand and could claim to be considered before that of heredity.[2] It is true that in the literature of the subject one occasionally comes across remarks upon precocious sexual activity in small children—upon erections, masturbation and even activities resembling coitus. But these are always quoted only as exceptional events, as oddities or as horrifying instances of precocious depravity. So far as I know, not a single author has clearly recognized the regular existence of a sexual instinct in childhood, and in the writings that have become so numerous on the development of children, the chapter on "Sexual Development" is as a rule omitted.[3]

INFANTILE AMNESIA

The reason for this strange neglect is to be sought, I think, partly in considerations of propriety, which the authors obey as a result of their own upbringing, and partly in a psychological phenomenon which has itself hitherto eluded explanation. What I have in mind is the peculiar amnesia which, in the case of most people, though by no means all, hides the earliest beginnings of their childhood up to their sixth or eighth year. Hitherto it has not occurred to us to feel any astonishment at the fact of this amnesia, though we might have had good grounds for doing so. For we learn from other people that during these years, of which at a later date we retain nothing in our memory but a few unintelligible and fragmentary recollections, we reacted in a lively manner to impressions, that we were capable of expressing pain and joy in a human fashion, that we gave evidence of love, jealousy and other passionate feelings by which we were strongly moved at the time, and even that we gave utterance to remarks which were regarded by adults as good evidence of our possessing insight and the beginnings of a capacity for judgement. And of all this we, when we are grown up, have no knowledge of our own! Why should our memory lag so far behind the other activities of our minds? We have, on the contrary, good reason to believe that there is no period at which the capacity for receiving and reproducing impressions is greater than precisely during the years of childhood.[4]

On the other hand we must assume, or we can convince ourselves by a psychological examination of other people, that the very same impressions that we have forgotten have none the less left the deepest traces on our minds and have had a determining effect upon the whole of our later development. There can, therefore, be no question of any real abolition of the impressions of childhood, but rather of an amnesia similar to that which neurotics exhibit for later events, and of which the essence consists in a simple withholding of these impressions from consciousness, viz., in their repression. But what are the forces which bring about this repression of the impressions of childhood? Whoever could solve this riddle would, I think, have explained *hysterical* amnesia as well.

Meanwhile we must not fail to observe that the existence of infantile amnesia provides a new point of comparison between the mental states of children and psychoneurotics. We have already come across another such point in the formula to which we were led, to the effect that the sexuality of psychoneurotics has remained at, or been carried back to, an infantile stage. Can it be, after all, that infantile amnesia, too, is brought into relation with the sexual impulses of childhood?

Moreover, the connection between infantile and hysterical amnesia is more than a mere play upon words. Hysterical amnesia, which occurs at the bidding of repression, is only explicable by the fact that the subject is already in possession of a store of memory-traces which have been withdrawn from conscious disposal, and which are now, by an associative link, attracting to themselves the material which the forces of repression are engaged in repelling from consciousness.[5] It may be said that without infantile amnesia there would be no hysterical amnesia.

I believe, then, that infantile amnesia, which turns everyone's childhood into something like a prehistoric epoch and conceals from him the beginnings of his own sexual life, is responsible for the fact that in general no importance is attached to childhood in the development of sexual life. The gaps in our knowledge which have arisen in this way cannot be bridged by a single observer. As long ago as in the year 1896 I insisted on the significance of the years of childhood in the origin of certain important phenomena connected with sexual life, and since then I have never ceased to emphasize the part played in sexuality by the infantile factor.

> The sexual life of children is pre-genital; this means that children, incapable of sexual orgasm, obtain strong pleasure through breast feeding, thumb-sucking, bowel movements, and manipulation of their genitals. While breast feeding and bowel movements are compelled, respectively, by the instinct for self-preservation and by bodily tension, a *distinct* instinct for pleasure attaches itself to these activities and demands frequent satisfaction. Think about your daily activities—you do not eat just to stay alive, but also for pleasure. How long can you go without other pleasurable activities? Contrast Freud's view of our original state with the Enlightenment belief that we *seek a rational* activity or work, monetary accumulation, community. For Freud, these rational acts are motivated by *ananke* (practicality); they are a sublimated[6] means to pleasure and security, but not our true, freely chosen, primary activity.

THUMB-SUCKING

For reasons which will appear later, I shall take thumb-sucking (or sensual sucking) as a sample of the sexual manifestations of childhood. . . .

Thumb-sucking appears already in early infancy and may continue into maturity, or even persist all through life. It consists in the rhythmic repetition of a sucking contact by the mouth (or lips). There is no question of the purpose of this procedure being the taking of nourishment. A portion of the lip itself, the tongue, or any other part of the skin within reach—even the big toe—may be taken as the object upon which this sucking is carried out. . . .

. . . In the nursery, sucking is often classed along with the other kinds of sexual "naughtiness" of children. This view has been most energetically repudiated by numbers of paediatricians and nerve-specialists, though this is no doubt partly due to a confusion between "sexual" and "genital." Their objection raises a difficult question and one which cannot be evaded: what is the general characteristic which enables us to recognize the sexual manifestations of children? The concatenation of phenomena into which we have been given an insight by psycho-analytic investigation justifies us, in my opinion, in regarding thumb-sucking as a sexual manifestation and in choosing it for our study of the essential features of infantile sexual activity.[7]

AUTO-EROTICISM

We are in duty bound to make a thorough examination of this example. It must be insisted that the most striking feature of this sexual activity is that the instinct is not directed towards other people, but obtains satisfaction from the subject's own body. It is "auto-erotic," to call it by a happily chosen term introduced by Havelock Ellis (1910).[8]

Furthermore, it is clear that the behaviour of a child who indulges in thumb-sucking is determined by a search for some pleasure which has already been experienced and is now remembered. In the simplest case he proceeds to find this satisfaction by sucking rhythmically at some part of the skin or mucous membrane. It is also easy to guess the occasions on which the child had his first experiences of the pleasure which he is now striving to renew. It was the child's first and most vital activity, his sucking at his mother's breast, or at substitutes for it, that must have familiarized him with this pleasure. The child's lips, in our view, behave like an erotogenic zone, and no doubt stimulation by the warm flow of milk is the cause of the pleasurable sensation. The satisfaction of the erotogenic zone is associated, in the first instance, with the satisfaction of the need for nourishment. To begin with, sexual activity attaches itself to functions serving the *purpose* of self-preservation and does not become independent of them until later. No one who has seen a baby sinking back satiated from the breast and falling asleep with flushed cheeks and a blissful smile can escape the reflection that this picture persists as a prototype of the expression of sexual satisfaction in later life. The need for repeating the sexual satisfaction now becomes detached from the need for taking nourishment—a separation which becomes inevitable when the teeth appear and food is no longer taken in only by sucking, but is also chewed up. The child does not make use of an extraneous body for his sucking, but prefers a part of his own skin because it is more convenient, because it makes him independent of the external world, which he is not yet able to control, and because in that way he provides himself, as it were, with a second erotogenic zone, though one of an inferior kind. The inferiority of this second region is among the reasons why at a later date he seeks the corresponding part—the lips—of another person. ("It's a pity I can't kiss myself," he seems to be saying.) . . .

Our study of thumb-sucking or sensual sucking has already given us the three essential characteristics of an infantile sexual manifestation. At its origin it attaches itself to one of the vital somatic functions; it has as yet no sexual object, and is thus auto-erotic; and its sexual aim is dominated by an erotogenic zone. It is to be anticipated that these characteristics will be found to apply equally to most of the other activities of the infantile sexual instincts.

THE INFANTILE SEXUAL AIM

The sexual aim of the infantile instinct consists in obtaining satisfaction by means of an appropriate stimulation of the erotogenic zone which has been selected in one way or another. This satisfaction must have been previously experienced in order to have left behind a need for its repetition; and we may expect that Nature will have made safe provisions so that this experience of satisfaction shall not be left to chance. We have already learnt what the contrivance is that fulfills this purpose in the case of the labial zone: it is the simultaneous connection which links this part of the body with the taking in of food. We shall come across other, similar contrivances as sources of sexuality. The state of being in need of a repetition of the satisfaction reveals itself in two ways: by a peculiar feeling of tension, possessing, rather, the character of un-pleasure, and by a sensation of itching or stimulation which is centrally conditioned and projected on to the peripheral erotogenic zone. We can therefore formulate a sex-ual aim in another way: it consists in replacing the projected sensation of stimulation in the erotogenic zone by an external stimulus which removes that sensation by pro-ducing a feeling of satisfaction. This external stimulus will usually consist in some kind of manipulation that is analogous to the sucking.

The fact that the need can also be evoked peripherally, by a real modification of the erotogenic zone, is in complete harmony with our physiological knowledge. This strikes us as somewhat strange only because, in order to remove one stimulus, it seems necessary to adduce a second one at the same spot.

> The sexual life of children and their adult lives are shaped by those who by caring for them also provide pleasure. However, the ways by which our major caregivers pro-vide care can result in barriers to happiness (neurosis), in childhood or in adulthood. A client of mine made this remark at the end of his therapy: "I'm addicted to drugs because my parents are addicted to me! Since my father drives me to the clinic every day, he may as well come in and drink the methadone[9] with me." Also, a number of years ago a student mentioned an acquaintance who did well (held down a job and stayed out of trouble) when the acquaintance and his wife were together, but quickly fell apart (lost his job and went on substance abuse binges) numerous times during their frequent split-ups. Read Freud's ideas on infantile anxiety and parental behavior and then consider both cases.

From The Transformations of Puberty

THE SEXUAL OBJECT DURING EARLY INFANCY

But even after sexual activity has become detached from the taking of nourishment, an important part of this first and most significant of all sexual relations is left over, which helps to prepare for the choice of an object and thus to restore the happiness that as been lost. All through the period of latency[10] children learn to feel for other people who help them in their helplessness and satisfy their needs a love which is on the model of, and a continuation of, their relation as sucklings to their nursing mother. There may perhaps be an inclination to dispute the possibility of identifying a child's affection and esteem for those who look after him with sexual love. I think, however, that a closer psychological examination may make it possible to establish this identity beyond any doubt. A child's intercourse with anyone responsible for his care affords him an unending source of sexual excitation and satisfaction from his erotogenic zones. This is especially so since the person in charge of him, who, after all, is as a rule his mother, herself regards him with feelings that are derived from her own sexual life: she strokes him, kisses him, rocks him and quite clearly treats him as a substitute for a complete sexual object.[11] A mother would probably be horrified if she were made aware that all her marks of affection were rousing her child's sexual instinct and preparing for its later intensity. She regards what she does as asexual, "pure" love, since, after all, she carefully avoids applying more excitations to the child's genitals than are unavoidable in nursery care. As we know, however, the sexual instinct is not aroused only by direct excitation of the genital zone. What we call affection will un-failingly show its effects one day on the genital zones as well. Moreover, if the mother understood more of the high importance of the part played by instincts in mental life as a whole—in all its ethical and psychical achievements—she would spare herself any self-reproaches even after her enlightenment. She is only fulfilling her task in teach-ing the child to love. After all, he is meant to grow up into a strong and capable per-son with vigorous sexual needs and to accomplish during his life all the things that human beings are urged to do by their instincts. It is true that an excess of parental af-fection does harm by causing precocious sexual maturity and also because, by spoil-ing the child, it makes him incapable in later life of temporarily doing without love or of being content with a smaller amount of it. One of the clearest indications that a child will later become neurotic is to be seen in an insatiable demand for his parents' affection. And on the other hand neuropathic parents, who are inclined as a rule to dis-play excessive affection, are precisely those who are most likely by their caresses to arouse the child's disposition to neurotic illness. Incidentally, this example shows that there are ways more direct than inheritance by which neurotic parents can hand their disorder on to their children.

INFANTILE ANXIETY

Children themselves behave from an early age as though their dependence on the people looking after them were in the nature of sexual love. Anxiety in children is originally nothing other than an expression of the fact that they are feeling the loss of the person they love. It is for this reason that they are frightened of every stranger. They are afraid in the dark because in the dark they cannot see the person they love; and their fear is soothed if they can take hold of that person's hand in the dark. To at-tribute to bogeys and blood-curdling stories told by nurses the responsibility for mak-ing children timid is to over-estimate their efficacy. The truth is merely that children who are inclined to be timid are affected by stories which would make no impression whatever upon others, and it is only children with a sexual instinct that is excessive or has developed prematurely or has become vociferous owing to too much petting who are inclined to be timid. In this respect a child, by turning his libido into anxiety when he cannot satisfy it, behaves like an adult. On the other hand an adult who has become neurotic owing to his libido being unsatisfied behaves in his anxiety like a child: he begins to be frightened when he is alone, that is to say when he is away from someone of whose love he had felt secure, and he seeks to assuage this fear by the most childish measures.[12]

> Like the mouth, the anus is also a pleasure zone for children and is not (though few of us may readily or publicly admit this) an uncommon adult erogenous zone. Genital stimulation is also common among children. So far, what emerges from Freud's views on the sexual life of children is the power of the natural, biologically driven activities of early life.

From Infantile Sexuality

ACTIVITY OF THE ANAL ZONE

Like the labial zone, the anal zone is well suited by its position to act as a medium through which sexuality may attach itself to other somatic functions. It is to be presumed that the erotogenic significance of this part of the body is very great from the first. We learn with some astonishment from psycho-analysis of the transmutations normally undergone by the sexual excitations arising from this zone and of the frequency with which it retains a considerable amount of susceptibility to genital stimulation throughout life. The intestinal disturbances which are so common in childhood see to it that the zone shall not lack intense excitations. Intestinal catarrhs at the tenderest age make children "nervy," as people say, and in cases of later neurotic illness they have a determining influence on the symptoms in which the neurosis is expressed, and they put at its disposal the whole range of intestinal disturbances. If we bear in mind the erotogenic significance of the outlet of the intestinal canal, which persists, at all events in a modified form, we shall not be inclined to scoff at the influence of haemorrhoids, to which old-fashioned medicine used to attach so much importance in explaining neurotic conditions.

Children who are making use of the susceptibility to erotogenic stimulation of the anal zone betray themselves by holding back their stool till its accumulation brings about violent muscular contractions and, as it passes through the anus, is able to produce powerful stimulation of the mucous membrane. In so doing it must no doubt cause not only painful but also highly pleasurable sensations. One of the clearest signs of subsequent eccentricity or nervousness is to be seen when a baby obstinately refuses to empty his bowels when he is put on the pot—that is, when his nurse wants him to—and holds back that function till he himself chooses to exercise it. He is naturally not concerned with dirtying the bed, he is only anxious not to miss the subsidiary pleasure attached to defaecating. Educators are once more right when they describe children who keep the process back as "naughty."

The contents of the bowels, which act as a stimulating mass upon a sexually sensitive portion of mucous membrane, behave like forerunners of another organ, which is destined to come into action after the phase of childhood. But they have other important meanings for the infant. They are clearly treated as a part of the infant's own body and represent his first "gift": by producing them he can express his active compliance with his environment and, by withholding them, his disobedience. From being a "gift" they later come to acquire the meaning of "baby"—for babies, according to one of the sexual theories of children, are acquired by eating and are born through the bowels.

The retention of the faecal mass, which is thus carried out intentionally by the child to begin with, in order to serve, as it were, as a masturbatory stimulus upon the anal zone or to be employed in his relation to the people looking after him, is also one of the roots of the constipation which is so common among neuropaths. Further, the whole significance of the anal zone is reflected in the fact that few neurotics are to be found without their special scatological practices, ceremonies, and so on, which they carefully keep secret.[13]

Actual masturbatory stimulation of the anal zone by means of the finger, provoked by a centrally determined or peripherally maintained sensation of itching, is by no means rare among older children.

ACTIVITY OF THE GENITAL ZONES

Among the erotogenic zones that form part of the child's body there is one which certainly does not play the opening part, and which cannot be the vehicle of the oldest sexual impulses, but which is destined to great things in the future. In both male and female children it is brought into connection with micturition (in the glans and clitoris) and in the former is enclosed in a pouch of mucous membrane, so that there can be no lack of stimulation of it by secretions which may give an early start to sexual excitation. The sexual activities of this erotogenic zone, which forms part of the sexual organs proper, are the beginning of what is later to become "normal" sexual life. The anatomical situation of this region, the secretions in which it is bathed, the washing and rubbing to which it is subjected in the course of a child's toilet, as well as accidental stimulation (such as the movement of intestinal worms in the case of girls), make it inevitable that the pleasurable feeling which this part of the body is capable of producing should be noticed by children even during their earliest infancy, and should give rise to a need for its repetition. If we consider this whole range of contrivances and bear in mind that both making a mess and measures for keeping clean are bound to operate in much the same way, it is scarcely possible to avoid the conclusion that the foundations for the future primacy over sexual activity exercised by this erotogenic zone are established by early infantile masturbation, which scarcely a single individual escapes. The action which disposes of the stimulus and brings about satisfaction consists in a rubbing movement with the hand or in the application of pressure (no doubt on the lines of a pre-existing reflex) either from the hand or by bringing the thighs together. This last method is by far the more common in the case of girls. The preference for the hand which is shown by boys is already evidence of the important contribution which the instinct for mastery is destined to make to masculine sexual activity.[14]

It will be in the interests of clarity if I say at once that three phases of infantile masturbation are to be distinguished. The first of these belongs to early infancy, and the second to the brief efflorescence of sexual activity about the fourth year of life; only the third phase corresponds to pubertal masturbation, which is often the only kind taken into account.

> The natural behavior of children runs up against the moral preferences of their culture. Ideally, male and female children learn that libidinal[15] attachments to their parents must be redirected. However, the impressions left in the psyche by how this situation is carried on—which could entail various permutations—reemerge in puberty and, if not resolved, in adulthood. For example, sexual impotence may be indicative of some unresolved aspect of a necessary libidinal detachment from one or both parents—something which *should* have begun in early childhood and reached a maturity in the teenage years. An interesting question emerges: Absent cultural taboos, would we *naturally* find incest to be morally and intellectually disgusting?

From The Transformations of Puberty

THE BARRIER AGAINST INCEST

We see, therefore, that the parents' affection for their child may awaken his sexual instinct prematurely (i.e. before the somatic conditions of puberty are present) to such a degree that the mental excitation breaks through in an unmistakable fashion to the genital system. If, on the other hand, they are fortunate enough to avoid this, then their affection can perform its task of directing the child in his choice of a sexual object when he reaches maturity. No doubt the simplest course for the child would be to choose as his sexual objects the same persons whom, since his childhood, he has loved with what may be described as damped-down libido. But, by the postponing of sexual maturation, time has been gained in which the child can erect, among other restraints on sexuality, the barrier against incest, and can thus take up into himself the moral precepts which expressly exclude from his object-choice, as being blood-relations, the persons whom he has loved in his childhood. Respect for this barrier is essentially a cultural demand made by society. Society must defend itself against the danger that the interests which it needs for the establishment of higher social units may be swallowed up by the family; and for this reason, in the case of every individual, but in particular of adolescent boys, it seeks by all possible means to loosen their connection with their family—a connection which, in their childhood, is the only important one.[16]

It is in the world of ideas, however, that the choice of an object is accomplished at first; and the sexual life of maturing youth is almost entirely restricted to indulging in phantasies, that is, in ideas that are not destined to be carried into effect.[17] In these phantasies the infantile tendencies invariably emerge once more, but this time with intensified pressure from somatic sources. Among these tendencies the first place is taken with uniform frequency by the child's sexual impulses towards his parents, which are as a rule already differentiated owing to the attraction of the opposite sex—the son being drawn towards his mother and the daughter towards her father. At the same time as these plainly incestuous phantasies are overcome and repudiated, one of the most significant, but also one of the most painful, psychical achievements of the pubertal period is completed: detachment from parental authority, a process that alone makes possible the *opposition* which is so important for the progress of civilization, between the new generation and the old. At every stage in the course of development through which all human beings ought by rights to pass, a certain number are held back; so there are some who have never got over their parents' authority and have withdrawn their affection from them either very incompletely or not at all. They are mostly girls, who, to the delight of their parents, have persisted in all their childish love far beyond puberty. It is most instructive to find that it is precisely these girls who in their later marriage lack the capacity to give their husbands what is due to them; they make cold wives and remain sexually unaesthetic. We learn from this that sexual love and what appears to be non-sexual love for parents are fed from the same sources; the latter, that is to say, merely corresponds to an infantile fixation of the libido.

The closer one comes to the deeper disturbances of psychosexual development, the more unmistakably the importance of incestuous object-choice emerges. In psychoneurotics a large portion or the whole of their psychosexual activity in finding an object remains in the unconscious as a result of their repudiation of sexuality. Girls with an exaggerated need for affection and an equally exaggerated horror of the real demands made by sexual life have an irresistible temptation on the one hand to realize the ideal of asexual love in their lives and on the other hand to conceal their libido behind an affection which they can express without self-reproaches, by holding fast throughout their lives to their infantile fondness, revived at puberty, for their parents or brothers and sisters. Psycho-analysis has no difficulty in showing persons of this kind that they are *in love*, in the everyday sense of the word, with these blood-relations of theirs; for, with the help of their symptoms and other manifestations of their illness, it traces their unconscious thoughts and translates them into conscious ones. In cases in which someone who has previously been healthy falls ill after an unhappy experience in love it is also possible to show with certainty that the mechanism of his illness consists in a turning-back of his libido on to those whom he preferred in his infancy.

AFTER-EFFECTS OF INFANTILE OBJECT-CHOICE

Even a person who has been fortunate enough to avoid an incestuous fixation of his libido does not entirely escape its influence. It often happens that a young man falls in love seriously for the first time with a mature woman, or a girl with an elderly man in a position of authority; this is clearly an echo of the phase of development that we have been discussing, since these figures are able to re-animate pictures of their mother or father. There can be no doubt that every object-choice whatever is based, though less closely, on these prototypes. A man, especially, looks for someone who can represent his picture of his mother, as it has dominated his mind from his earliest childhood; and accordingly, if his mother is still alive, she may well resent this new version of herself and meet her with hostility. In view of the importance of a child's relations to his parents in determining his later choice of a sexual object, it can easily be understood that any disturbance of those relations will produce the gravest effects upon his adult sexual life. Jealousy in a lover is never without an infantile root or at least an infantile reinforcement. If there are quarrels between the parents or if their marriage is unhappy, the ground will be prepared in their children for the severest predisposition to a disturbance of sexual development or to a neurotic illness.

A child's affection for his parents is no doubt the most important infantile trace which, after being revived at puberty, points the way to his choice of an object; but it is not the only one. Other starting-points with the same early origin enable a man to develop more than one sexual line, based no less upon his childhood, and to lay down very various conditions for his object-choice.

> The weight attached by parents, relatives, peers, and others to cultural preferences leaves its mark on the child's continuing mental and emotional development. The child has learned—to varying degrees in individual cases, and in some abnormal family environments not at all—to redirect her or his sexual feelings to other activities (sublimation). Biological drives, originally acting on their own, now compete with social learning. The result—again, varying in individual cases—is the child's forced identification with the "intruder" (ideas of right and wrong) and her or his incorporation of these ideas (reaction-formation).

From Infantile Sexuality

THE PERIOD OF SEXUAL LATENCY IN CHILDHOOD
AND ITS INTERRUPTIONS

The remarkably frequent reports of what are described as irregular and exceptional sexual impulses in childhood, as well as the uncovering in neurotics of what have hitherto been unconscious memories of childhood, allow us to sketch out the sexual occurrences of that period in some such way as this.[18]

There seems no doubt that germs of sexual impulses are already present in the new-born child and that these continue to develop for a time, but are then overtaken by a progressive process of suppression; this in turn is itself interrupted by periodical advances in sexual development or may be held up by individual *peculiarities*. Nothing is known for certain concerning the regularity and periodicity of this oscillating course of development. It seems, however, that the sexual life of children usually emerges in a form accessible to observation round about the third or fourth year of life.

SEXUAL INHIBITIONS

It is during this period of total or only partial latency that are built up the mental forces which are later to impede the course of the sexual instinct and, like dams, restrict its flow—disgust, feelings of shame and the claims of aesthetic and moral ideals. One gets an impression from civilized children that the construction of these dams is a product of education, and no doubt education has much to do with it. But in reality this development is organically determined and fixed by heredity, and it can occasionally occur without any help at all from education. Education will not be trespassing beyond its appropriate domain if it limits itself to following the lines which have already been laid down organically and to impressing them somewhat more clearly and deeply.

REACTION-FORMATION AND SUBLIMATION

What is it that goes to the making of these constructions which are so important for the growth of a civilized and normal individual? They probably emerge at the cost of the infantile sexual impulses themselves. Thus the activity of those impulses does not cease even during this period of latency, though their energy is diverted, wholly or in great part, from their sexual use and directed to other ends. Historians of civilization appear to be at one in assuming that powerful components are acquired for every kind of cultural achievement by this diversion of sexual instinctual forces from sexual aims and their direction to new ones—a process which deserves the name of "sublimation." To this we would add, accordingly, that the same process plays a part in the development of the individual and we would place its beginning in the period of sexual latency of childhood.

It is possible further to form some idea of the mechanism of this process of sublimation. On the one hand, it would seem, the sexual impulses cannot be utilized during these years of childhood, since the reproductive functions have been deferred—a fact which constitutes the main feature of the period of latency. On the other hand, these impulses would seem in themselves to be perverse—that is, to arise from erotogenic zones and to derive their activity from instincts which, in view of the direction of the subject's development, can only arouse unpleasurable feelings. They consequently evoke opposing mental forces (reacting impulses) which, in order to suppress this unpleasure, effectively build up the mental dams that I have already mentioned—disgust, shame and morality.

INTERRUPTIONS OF THE LATENCY PERIOD

We must not deceive ourselves as to the hypothetical nature and insufficient clarity of our knowledge concerning the processes of the infantile period of latency or deferment; but we shall be on firmer ground in pointing out that such an application of infantile sexuality represents an educational ideal from which individual development usually diverges at some point and often to a considerable degree. From time to time a fragmentary manifestation of sexuality which has evaded sublimation may break through; or some sexual activity may persist through the whole duration of the latency period until the sexual instinct emerges with greater intensity at puberty. In so far as educators pay any attention at all to infantile sexuality, they behave exactly as though they shared our views as to the construction of the moral defensive forces at the cost of sexuality, and as though they knew that sexual activity makes a child uneducable: for they stigmatize every sexual manifestation by children as a "vice," without being able to do much against it. We, on the other hand, have every reason for turning our attention to these phenomena which are so much dreaded by education, for we may expect them to help us to discover the original configuration of the sexual instincts.

> Up to this point the individual has incorporated into his or her psyche thoughts, feelings, relationships, and preferences. The onset of puberty compels him or her to find an external object for release of sexual tensions. Still, the experiences and powerful impressions of the previous years are not rendered meaningless. The *biologically* driven sexual aims of the adolescent and adult will be realized or not, according to where the individual is *psychologically;* what we have experienced, whether "normal" or problematic, will reemerge. It is quite possible that some persons are fixated—stuck in an unconscious early situation (memory)—and encounter barriers to social, professional, and sexual gratification.

From The Transformations of Puberty

With the arrival of puberty, changes set in which are destined to give infantile sexual life its final, normal shape. The sexual instinct has hitherto been predominantly auto-erotic; it now finds a sexual object. Its activity has hitherto been derived from a number of separate instincts and erotogenic zones, which, independently of one another, have pursued a certain sort of pleasure as their sole sexual aim. Now, however, a new sexual aim appears, and all the component instincts combine to attain it, while the erotogenic zones become subordinated to the primacy of the genital zone. Since the new sexual aim assigns very different functions to the two sexes, their sexual development now diverges greatly. That of males is the more straightforward and the more understandable, while that of females actually enters upon a kind of involution. A normal sexual life is only assured by an exact convergence of the affectionate current and the sensual current both being directed towards the sexual object and sexual aim. (The former, the affectionate current, comprises what remains over of the infantile efflorescence of sexuality.) It is like the completion of a tunnel which has been driven through a hill from both directions.

The new sexual aim in men consists in the discharge of the sexual products. The earlier one, the attainment of pleasure, is by no means alien to it; on the contrary, the highest degree of pleasure is attached to this final act of the sexual process. The sexual instinct is now subordinated to the reproductive function; it becomes, so to say, altruistic. If this transformation is to succeed, the original dispositions and all the other characteristics of the instincts must be taken into account in the process. Just as on any other occasion on which the organism should by rights make new combinations and adjustments leading to complicated mechanisms, here too there are possibilities of pathological disorders if these new arrangements are not carried out. Every pathological disorder of sexual life is rightly to be regarded as an inhibition in development.

THE FINDING OF AN OBJECT

The processes at puberty thus establish the primacy of the genital zones; and, in a man, the penis, which has now become capable of erection, presses forward insistently towards the new sexual aim—penetration into a cavity in the body which excites his genital zone. Simultaneously on the psychical side the process of finding an object, for which preparations have been made from earliest childhood, is completed. At a time at which the first beginnings of sexual satisfaction are still linked with the taking of nourishment, the sexual instinct has a sexual object outside the infant's own body in the shape of his mother's breast. It is only later that the instinct loses that object, just at the time, perhaps, when the child is able to form a total idea of the person to whom the organ that is giving him satisfaction belongs. As a rule the sexual instinct then becomes auto-erotic, and not until the period of latency has been passed through is the original relation restored. There are thus good reasons why a child sucking at his mother's breast has become the prototype of every relation of love. The finding of an object is in fact a refinding of it.

Jokes and Their Relation to the Unconscious

The preceding essays on sexuality suggest that the instincts present at birth, for adults, reside mainly in the unconscious; Freud's work on jokes is grounded in this theory.

Serenissimus[1] asked a stranger by whose similarity to his own person he had been struck: "Was your mother in the Palace at one time?" and the repartee was: "No, but my father was." The person to whom the question was put would no doubt have liked to knock down the impertinent individual who dared by such an allusion to cast a slur on his beloved mother's memory. But the impertinent individual was Serenissimus, whom one may not knock down or even insult unless one is prepared to purchase that revenge at the price of one's whole existence. The insult must therefore, it would seem, be swallowed in silence. But fortunately a joke shows the way in which the insult may be safely avenged—by making use of the technical method of unification in order to take up the allusion and turn it back against the aggressor. . . .

"Pleasure in nonsense," as we may call it for short, is concealed in serious life to a vanishing point. . . . During the period in which a child is learning how to handle the vocabulary of his mother-tongue, it gives him obvious pleasure to "experiment with it in play," to use Groos's words. And he puts words together without regard to the condition that they should make sense, in order to obtain from them the pleasurable effect of rhythm or rhyme. Little by little he is forbidden this enjoyment, till all that remains permitted to him are significant combinations of words. But when he is older attempts still emerge at disregarding the restrictions that have been learnt on the use of words. Words are disfigured by particular little additions being made to them, their

The excerpts in this section are taken from *Jokes and Their Relation to the Unconscious* by Sigmund Freud, translated by James Strachey. Copyright © 1960 by James Strachey, renewed 1988 by Alix Strachey. Used by permission of W. W. Norton & Company, Inc.

forms are altered by certain manipulations (e.g. by reduplications or *"Zittersprache"*[2]), or a private language may even be constructed for use among playmates. These attempts are found again among certain categories of mental patients.

Whatever the motive may have been which led the child to begin these games, I believe that in his later development he gives himself up to them with the consciousness that they are nonsensical, and that he finds enjoyment in the attraction of what is forbidden by reason. He now uses games in order to withdraw from the pressure of critical reason. But there is far more potency in the restrictions which must establish themselves in the course of a child's education in logical thinking and in distinguishing between what is true and false in reality; and for this reason the rebellion against the compulsion of logic and reality is deep-going and long-lasting. Even the phenomena of imaginative activity must be included in this [rebellious] category. The power of criticism has increased so greatly in the later part of childhood and in the period of learning which extends over puberty that the pleasure in "liberated nonsense" only seldom dares to show itself directly. One does not venture to say anything absurd. But the characteristic tendency of boys to do absurd or silly things seems to me to be directly derived from the pleasure of nonsense. In pathological cases we often see this tendency so far intensified that once more it dominates the schoolboy's talk and answers. I have been able to convince myself in the case of a few boys of secondary school age who had developed neuroses that the unconscious workings of their pleasure in the nonsense they produced played no less a part in their inefficiency than did their real ignorance. . . .

. . . For the euphoria which we endeavour to reach by these means [jokes] is nothing other than the mood of a period of life in which we were accustomed to deal with our psychical work in general with a small expenditure of energy—the mood of our childhood, when we were ignorant of the comic, when we were incapable of jokes and when we had no need of humour to make us feel happy in our life.

The Ego and the Id

The previous readings illustrate Freud's theory that neurosis occurring in adolescence or adulthood entailed a fixation or return to the individual's forgotten earlier traumas. We can perhaps better understand the nature of neurosis by exploring the psychoanalytic theorization of the psyche. Each of us is an independent self (ego), and our ego interacts not only with the external but also with our internal world. However, the ego is also a *part* of our internal world. Psychoanalysis sought to isolate the distinct parts of this internal structure and to explain their interactions.

THE EGO AND THE ID

Pathological research has directed our interest too exclusively to the repressed. We should like to learn more about the ego, now that we know that it, too, can be unconscious in the proper sense of the word. Hitherto the only guide we have had during our investigations has been the distinguishing mark of being conscious or unconscious; we have finally come to see how ambiguous this can be.

Now all our knowledge is invariably bound up with consciousness. We can come to know even the *Ucs.* [unconscious] only by making it conscious. But stop, how is that possible? What does it mean when we say "making something conscious"? How can that come about?

We already know the point from which we have to start in this connection. We have said that consciousness is the *surface* of the mental apparatus; that is, we have ascribed it as a function to a system which is spatially the first one reached from the external world—and spatially not only in the functional sense but, on this occasion, also in the sense of anatomical dissection. Our investigations too must take this perceiving surface as a starting-point.

The excerpts in this section are taken from *The Ego and the Id* by Sigmund Freud, translated by James Strachey. Copyright © 1960 by James Strachey, renewed 1988 by Alix Strachey. Used by permission of W. W. Norton & Company, Inc.

All perceptions which are received from without (sense-perceptions) and from within—what we call sensations and feelings—are Cs. [conscious] from the start. But what about those internal processes which we may—roughly and inexactly—sum up under the name of thought-processes? They represent displacements of mental energy which are effected somewhere in the interior of the apparatus as this energy proceeds on its way towards action. Do they advance to the surface, which causes consciousness to be generated? Or does consciousness make its way to them? This is clearly one of the difficulties that arise when one begins to take the spatial or "topographical"[1] idea of mental life seriously. Both these possibilities are equally unimaginable; there must be a third alternative.

I have already, in another place,[2] suggested that the real difference between an Ucs. and a Pcs. [preconscious] idea (thought) consists in this: that the former is carried out on some material which remains unknown, whereas the latter (the Pcs.) is in addition brought into connection with word-presentations. This is the first attempt to indicate distinguishing marks for the two systems, the Pcs. and the Ucs., other than their relation to consciousness. The question, "How does a thing become conscious?" would thus be more advantageously stated: "How does a thing become preconscious?" And the answer would be: "Through becoming connected with the word-presentations corresponding to it."

These word-presentations are residues of memories; they were at one time perceptions, and like all mnemic residues they can become conscious again. Before we concern ourselves further with their nature, it dawns upon us like a new discovery that only something which has once been a Cs. perception can become conscious, and that anything arising from within (apart from feelings) that seeks to become conscious must try to transform itself into external perceptions: this becomes possible by means of memory-traces.

> Since we have previously explored the urges which dominate early life and the processes of repression, we now turn to these interactions within the adult psyche. In the next passage, Freud seems to be placing the reader in the unconscious while looking outward and exploring what is there. This exploration of internal thoughts and sensations includes whether or not, and how, some of these become conscious. The concepts of id and ego emerge from this discussion. However, are the id and ego so clearly demarcated and distinct? Think back to Freud's depiction of infantile experiences. Do you think the ego exists prior to or emerges out of the id?

To return to our argument: if, therefore, this is the way in which something that is in itself unconscious becomes preconscious, the question how we make something that is repressed (pre)conscious would be answered as follows. It is done by supplying Pcs. intermediate links through the work of analysis. Consciousness remains where it is, therefore; but, on the other hand, the Ucs. does not rise into the Cs.

Whereas the relation of *external* perceptions to the ego is quite perspicuous, that of *internal* perceptions to the ego requires special investigation. It gives rise once more to a doubt whether we are really right in referring the whole of consciousness to the single superficial system *Pcpt.-Cs.* [perception and its occurrence with consciousness].

Internal perceptions yield sensations of processes arising in the most diverse and certainly also in the deepest strata of the mental apparatus. Very little is known about these sensations and feelings; those belonging to the pleasure-unpleasure series may still be regarded as the best examples of them. They are more primordial, more elementary, than perceptions arising externally and they can come about even when consciousness is clouded. . . .

Sensations of a pleasurable nature have not anything inherently impelling about them, whereas unpleasurable ones have it in the highest degree. The latter impel towards change, towards discharge, and that is why we interpret unpleasure as implying a heightening and pleasure a lowering of energic cathexis. Let us call what becomes conscious as pleasure and unpleasure a quantitative and qualitative "something" in the course of mental events; the question then is whether this "something" can become conscious in the place where it is, or whether it must first be transmitted to the system *Pcpt.*

Clinical experience decides for the latter. It shows us that this "something" behaves like a repressed impulse. It can exert driving force without the ego noticing the compulsion. Not until there is resistance to the compulsion, a hold-up in the discharge-reaction, does the "something" at once become conscious as unpleasure. In the same way that tensions arising from physical needs can remain unconscious, so also can pain—a thing intermediate between external and internal perception, which behaves like an internal perception even when its source is in the external world. It remains true, therefore, that sensations and feelings, too, only become conscious through reaching the system *Pcpt.*; if the way forward is barred, they do not come into being as sensations, although the "something" that corresponds to them in the course of excitation is the same as if they did. We then come to speak, in a condensed and not entirely correct manner, of "unconscious feelings," keeping up an analogy with unconscious ideas which is not altogether justifiable. Actually the difference is that, whereas with *Ucs. ideas* connecting links must be created before they can be brought into the *Cs.*, with *feelings*, which are themselves transmitted directly, this does not occur. In other words: the distinction between *Cs.* and *Pcs.* has no meaning where feelings are concerned; the *Pcs.* here drops out—and feelings are either conscious or unconscious. Even when they are attached to word-presentations, their becoming conscious is not due to that circumstance, but they become so directly.

The part played by word-presentations now becomes perfectly clear. By their interposition internal thought-processes are made into perceptions. It is like a demonstration of the theorem that all knowledge has its origin in external perception. When a hypercathexis of the process of thinking takes place, thoughts are *actually* perceived—as if they came from without—and are consequently held to be true.

After this clarifying of the relations between external and internal in the superficial system *Pcpt.-Cs.*, we can go on to work out our idea of the ego. It starts out, as we see, from the system *Pcpt.*, which is its nucleus, and begins by embracing the *Pcs.*, which is adjacent to the mnemic residues. But, as we have learnt, the ego is also unconscious.

Now I think we shall gain a great deal by following the suggestion of a writer who, from personal motives, vainly asserts that he has nothing to do with the rigours of pure science. I am speaking of Georg Groddeck, who is never tired of insisting that what we call our ego behaves essentially passively in life, and that, as he expresses it, we are "lived" by unknown and uncontrollable forces.[3] We have all had impressions of the same kind, even though they may not have overwhelmed us to the exclusion of all others, and we need feel no hesitation in finding a place for Groddeck's discovery in the structure of science. I propose to take it into account by calling the entity which starts out from the system *Pcpt.* and begins by being *Pcs.* the "ego," and by following Groddeck in calling the other part of the mind, into which this entity extends and which behaves as though it were *Ucs.*, the "id."

> Georg Groddeck, a physician who practiced therapy that resembled psychoanalysis and whom Freud often defended, viewed the ego as controlled by very powerful and mysterious forces. However, Freud theorized that these energies not only taunt the ego and cajole it to seek pleasure but also may influence us to perform in the opposite way.

The relation of the ego to consciousness has been entered into repeatedly, yet there are some important facts in this connection which remain to be described here. Accustomed as we are to taking our social or ethical scale of values along with us wherever we go, we feel no surprise at hearing that the scene of the activities of the lower passions is in the unconscious; we expect, moreover, that the higher any mental function ranks in our scale of values the more easily it will find access to consciousness assured to it. Here, however, psycho-analytic experience disappoints us. On the one hand, we have evidence that even subtle and difficult intellectual operations which ordinarily require strenuous reflection can equally be carried out preconsciously and without coming into consciousness. Instances of this are quite incontestable; they may occur, for example, during the state of sleep, as is shown when someone finds immediately after waking that he knows the solution to a difficult mathematical or other problem with which he had been wrestling in vain the day before.

There is another phenomenon, however, which is far stranger. In our analyses we discover that there are people in whom the faculties of self-criticism and conscience—mental activities, that is, that rank as extremely high ones—are unconscious and unconsciously produce effects of the greatest importance; the example of resistance remaining unconscious during analysis is therefore by no means unique. But this new discovery, which compels us, in spite of our better critical judgement, to speak of an "unconscious sense of guilt," bewilders us far more than the other and sets us fresh problems, especially when we gradually come to see that in a great number of neuroses an unconscious sense of guilt of this kind plays a decisive economic[4] part and puts the most powerful obstacles in the way of recovery. If we come back once more to our scale of values, we shall have to say that not only what is lowest but also what is highest in the ego can be unconscious. It is as if we were thus supplied with a proof of what we have just asserted of the conscious ego: that it is first and foremost a body-ego.

> How is it possible that the mind, dominated by primitive urges, could reject those urges? Understanding the mind requires that we step back and think about what the ego encounters. As much as psychoanalysis explicates, at the time, virtually uncharted *mental* terrain, the ego develops out of external circumstances interacting with bio-logical urges. A central event, the Oedipus complex, provides insights into not only the ego's rejection of the id's desires but also its resentment of that abandonment. Can we hold opposed feelings for an event or object? According to psychoanalysis, the nature of the early triangular relationship involving mother, father, and child will have life-long repercussions that are positive or negative, or *both*.

THE EGO AND THE SUPER-EGO (EGO IDEAL)

If the ego were merely the part of the id modified by the influence of the perceptual system, the representative in the mind of the real external world, we should have a simple state of things to deal with. But there is a further complication.

The considerations that led us to assume the existence of a grade in the ego, a dif-ferentiation within the ego, which may be called the "ego ideal" or "super-ego," have been stated elsewhere. They still hold good. The fact that this part of the ego is less firmly connected with consciousness is the novelty which calls for explanation.

At this point we must widen our range a little. We succeeded in explaining the painful disorder of melancholia by supposing that [in those suffering from it] an object which was lost has been set up again inside the ego—that is, that an object-cathexis[5] has been replaced by an identification. At that time, however, we did not appreciate the full significance of this process and did not know how common and how typical it is. Since then we have come to understand that this kind of substitution has a great share in determining the form taken by the ego and that it makes an essential contri-bution towards building up what is called its "character."

At the very beginning, in the individual's primitive oral phase, object-cathexis and identification are no doubt indistinguishable from each other. We can only suppose that later on object-cathexes proceed from the id, which feels erotic trends as needs. The ego, which to begin with is still feeble, becomes aware of the object-cathexes, and either acquiesces in them or tries to fend them of by the process of repression.[6]

When it happens that a person has to give up a sexual object, there quite often en-sues an alteration of his ego which can only be described as a setting up of the object inside the ego, as it occurs in melancholia; the exact nature of this substitution is as yet unknown to us. It may be that by this introjection, which is a kind of regression to the mechanism of the oral phase, the ego makes it easier for the object to be given up or renders that process possible. It may be that this identification is the sole condition under which the id can give up its objects. At any rate the process, especially in the early phases of development, is a very frequent one, and it makes it possible to suppose that the character of the ego is a precipitate of abandoned object-cathexes and that it contains the history of those object-choices. It must, of course, be admitted from the outset that there are varying degrees of capacity for resistance, which decide the extent to which a person's character fends off or accepts the influences of the history of his erotic object-choices. In women who have had many experiences in love there seems to be no difficulty in finding vestiges of their object-cathexes in the traits of their character. We must also take into consideration cases of simultaneous object-cathexis and identification—cases, that is, in which the alteration in character occurs before the object has been given up. In such cases the alteration in character has been able to survive the object-relation and in a certain sense to conserve it.

From another point of view it may be said that this transformation of an erotic object-choice into an alteration of the ego is also a method by which the ego can obtain control over the id and deepen its relations with it—at the cost, it is true, of acquiescing to a large extent in the id's experiences. When the ego assumes the features of the object, it is forcing itself, so to speak, upon the id as a love-object and is trying to make good the id's loss by saying: "Look, you can love me too—I am so like the object." . . .

Although it is a digression from our aim, we cannot avoid giving our attention for a moment longer to the ego's object-identifications. If they obtain the upper hand and become too numerous, unduly powerful and incompatible with one another, a pathological outcome will not be far off. It may come to a disruption of the ego in consequence of the different identifications becoming cut off from one another by resistances; perhaps the secret of the cases of what is described as "multiple personality" is that the different identifications seize hold of consciousness in turn. Even when things do not go so far as this, there remains the question of conflicts between the various identifications into which the ego comes apart, conflicts which cannot after all be described as entirely pathological.

But, whatever the character's later capacity for resisting the influences of abandoned object-cathexes may turn out to be, the effects of the first identifications made in earliest childhood will be general and lasting. This leads us back to the origin of the ego ideal; for behind it there lies hidden an individual's first and most important identification, his identification with the father in his own personal prehistory.[7] This is apparently not in the first instance the consequence or outcome of an object-cathexis; it is a direct and immediate identification and takes place earlier than any object-cathexis. But the object-choices belonging to the first sexual period and relating to the father and mother seem normally to find their outcome in an identification of this kind, and would thus reinforce the primary one.

The whole subject, however, is so complicated that it will be necessary to go into it in greater detail. The intricacy of the problem is due to two factors: the triangular character of the Oedipus situation and the constitutional bisexuality of each individual.

In its simplified form the case of a male child may be described as follows. At a very early age the little boy develops an object-cathexis for his mother, which originally related to the mother's breast and is the prototype of an object-choice on the anaclitic[8] model; the boy deals with his father by identifying himself with him. For a time these two relationships proceed side by side, until the boy's sexual wishes in regard to his mother become more intense and his father is perceived as an obstacle to them; from this the Oedipus complex originates. His identification with his father then takes on a hostile colouring and changes into a wish to get rid of his father in order to take his place with his mother. Henceforward his relation to his father is ambivalent; it seems as if the ambivalence inherent in the identification from the beginning had become manifest. An ambivalent attitude to his father and an object-relation of a solely affectionate kind to his mother make up the content of the simple positive Oedipus complex in a boy.

Along with the demolition of the Oedipus complex, the boy's object-cathexis of his mother must be given up. Its place may be filled by one of two things: either an identification with his mother or an intensification of his identification with his father. We are accustomed to regard the latter outcome as the more normal; it permits the affectionate relation to the mother to be in a measure retained. In this way the dissolution of the Oedipus complex would consolidate the masculinity in a boy's character. In a precisely analogous way, the outcome of the Oedipus attitude in a little girl may be an intensification of her identification with her mother (or the setting up of such an identification for the first time)—a result which will fix the child's feminine character.

These identifications are not what we should have expected, since they do not introduce the abandoned object into the ego; but this alternative outcome may also occur, and is easier to observe in girls than in boys. Analysis very often shows that a little girl, after she has had to relinquish her father as a love-object, will bring her masculinity into prominence and identify herself with her father (that is, with the object which has been lost), instead of with her mother. This will clearly depend on whether the masculinity in her disposition—whatever that may consist in—is strong enough.

It would appear, therefore, that in both sexes the relative strength of the masculine and feminine sexual dispositions is what determines whether the outcome of the Oedipus situation shall be an identification with the father or with the mother. This is one of the ways in which bisexuality takes a hand in the subsequent vicissitudes of the Oedipus complex. The other way is even more important. For one gets an impression that the simple Oedipus complex is by no means its commonest form, but rather represents a simplification or schematization which, to be sure, is often enough justified for practical purposes. Closer study usually discloses the more complete Oedipus complex, which is twofold, positive and negative, and is due to the bisexuality originally present in children: that is to say, a boy has not merely an ambivalent attitude towards his father and an affectionate object-choice towards his mother, but at the same time he also behaves like a girl and displays an affectionate feminine attitude to his father and a corresponding jealousy and hostility towards his mother. It is this complicating element introduced by bisexuality that makes it so difficult to obtain a clear view of the facts in connection with the earliest object-choices and identifications, and still more difficult to describe them intelligibly. It may even be that the ambivalence displayed in the relations to the parents should be attributed entirely to bisexuality and that it is not, as I have represented above, developed out of identification in consequence of rivalry.

In my opinion it is advisable in general, and quite especially where neurotics are concerned, to assume the existence of the complete Oedipus complex. Analytic experience then shows that in a number of cases one or the other constituent disappears, except for barely distinguishable traces; so that the result is a series with the normal positive Oedipus complex at one end and the inverted negative one at the other, while its intermediate members exhibit the complete form with one or other of its two components preponderating. At the dissolution of the Oedipus complex the four trends of which it consists will group themselves in such a way as to produce a father-identification and a mother-identification. The father-identification will preserve the object-relation to the mother which belonged to the positive complex and will at the same time replace the object-relation to the father which belonged to the inverted complex: and the same will be true, *mutatis mutandis,*[9] of the mother-identification. The relative intensity of the two identifications in any individual will reflect the preponderance in him of one or other of the two sexual dispositions.

> The result of the Oedipus complex is the creation of an ideal ego, or super-ego. We may then pursue a "moral" life with the same aggressive energy with which our libidinal urges seek pleasure. Yet, as later readings will suggest, a rigid reaction-formation[10] to the Oedipal event may be harmful.

The super-ego is, however, not simply a residue of the earliest object-choices of the id; it also represents an energetic reaction-formation against those choices. Its relation to the ego is not exhausted by the precept: "You *ought to be* like this (like your father)." It also comprises the prohibition: "You *may not be* like this (like your father)—that is, you may not do all that he does; some things are his prerogative." This double aspect of the ego ideal derives from the fact that the ego ideal had the task of repressing the Oedipus complex; indeed, it is to that revolutionary event that it owes its existence. Clearly the repression of the Oedipus complex was no easy task. The child's parents, and especially his father, were perceived as the obstacle to a realization of his Oedipus wishes; so his infantile ego fortified itself for the carrying out of the repression by erecting this same obstacle within itself. It borrowed strength to do this, so to speak, from the father, and this loan was an extraordinarily momentous act. The super-ego retains the character of the father, while the more powerful the Oedipus complex was and the more rapidly it succumbed to repression (under the influence of authority, religious teaching, schooling and reading), the stricter will be the domination of the super-ego over the ego later on—in the form of conscience or perhaps of an unconscious sense of guilt. I shall presently bring forward a suggestion about the source of its power to dominate in this way—the source, that is, of its compulsive character which manifests itself in the form of a categorical imperative.[11]

Some Psychical Consequences of the Anatomical Distinction Between the Sexes

The Oedipus complex is significant in the personality development of women but contains different features from that of a man. For both genders, anatomical realities play major roles in the Oedipal situation, character formation, and sexual behavior. Individuals' environmental conditions are by no means similar, and Freud accepts a varying range of reactions to such conditions, but the most basic (some will argue the only non-acquired) differences are highly influential for men and women.

In little girls the Oedipus complex raises one problem more than in boys. In both cases the mother is the original object; and there is no surprise that boys retain that object in the Oedipus complex. But how does it happen that girls abandon it and instead take their father as object? In pursuing this question I have been able to reach some conclusions which may throw light precisely on the prehistory of the Oedipus relation in girls.

Every analyst has come across certain women who cling with especial intensity and tenacity to the bond with their father and to the wish in which it culminates of having a child by him. We have good reason to suppose that the same wishful phantasy was also the motive force of their infantile masturbation, and it is easy to form an impression that at this point we have been brought up against an elementary and unanalysable fact of infantile sexual life. But a thorough analysis of these very cases brings something different to light—namely, that here the Oedipus complex has a long prehistory and is in some respects a secondary formation.

The excerpts in this section are taken from Sigmund Freud's *Some Psychical Consequences of the Anatomical Distinction Between the Sexes*, edited and translated by James Strachey, in *Standard Edition of the Complete Psychological Works of Sigmund Freud*, Vol. 19 (London: Hogarth Press and Institute of Psycho-Analysis, 1961), pp. 251–256, by arrangement with Paterson Marsh Ltd., London.

The old paediatrician Lindner [1879] once remarked that a child discovers the genital zones (the penis or the clitoris) as a source of pleasure while indulging in sensual sucking (thumb-sucking). I shall leave it an open question whether it is really true that the child takes the newly found source of pleasure in exchange for the recent loss of the mother's nipple—a possibility to which later phantasies (fellatio) seem to point. Be that as it may, the genital zone is discovered at some time or other, and there seems no justification for attributing any psychical content to the first activities in connection with it. But the first step in the phallic phase which begins in this way is not the linking-up of the masturbation with the object-cathexes of the Oedipus complex, but a momentous discovery which little girls are destined to make. They notice the penis of a brother or playmate, strikingly visible and of large proportions, at once recognize it as the superior counterpart of their own small and inconspicuous organ, and from that time forward fall a victim to envy for the penis.

There is an interesting contrast between the behaviour of the two sexes. In the analogous situation, when a little boy first catches sight of a girl's genital region, he begins by showing irresolution and lack of interest; he sees nothing or disavows what he has seen; he softens it down or looks about for expedients for bringing it into line with his expectations. It is not until later, when some threat of castration has obtained a hold upon him, that the observation becomes important to him: if he then recollects or repeats it. It arouses a terrible storm of emotion in him and forces him to believe in the reality of the threat which he has hitherto laughed at. This combination of circumstances leads to two reactions, which may become fixed and will in that case, whether separately or together or in conjunction with other factors, permanently determine the boy's relations to women: horror of the mutilated creature or triumphant contempt for her. These developments, however, belong to the future, though not to a very remote one.

A little girl behaves differently. She makes her judgement and her decision in a flash. She has seen it and knows that she is without it and wants to have it.[1]

Here what has been named the masculinity complex of women branches off. It may put great difficulties in the way of their regular development towards femininity, if it cannot be got over soon enough. The hope of some day obtaining a penis in spite of everything and so of becoming like a man may persist to an incredibly late age and may become a motive for strange and otherwise unaccountable actions. Or again, a process may set in which I should like to call a "disavowal," a process which in the mental life of children seems neither uncommon nor very dangerous but which in an adult would mean the beginning of a psychosis. Thus a girl may refuse to accept the fact of being castrated, may harden herself in the conviction that she does possess a penis, and may subsequently be compelled to behave as though she were a man.

The psychical consequences of envy for the penis, in so far as it does not become absorbed in the reaction-formation of the masculinity complex, are various and far-reaching. After a woman has become aware of the wound to her narcissism, she develops, like a scar, a sense of inferiority. When she has passed beyond her first attempt at explaining her lack of a penis as being a punishment personal to herself and has realized that that sexual character is a universal one, she begins to share the contempt felt by men for a sex which is the lesser in so important a respect, and, at least in holding that opinion, insists on being like a man.[2]

Even after penis-envy has abandoned its true object, it continues to exist: by an easy displacement it persists in the character-trait of *jealousy*. Of course, jealousy is not limited to one sex and has a wider foundation than this, but I am of opinion that it plays a far larger part in the mental life of women than of men and that that is because it is enormously reinforced from the direction of displaced penis-envy. While I was still unaware of this source of jealousy and was considering the phantasy "a child is being beaten," which occurs so commonly in girls, I constructed a first phase for it in which its meaning was that another child, a rival of whom the subject was jealous, was to be beaten. This phantasy seems to be a relic of the phallic period in girls. The peculiar rigidity which struck me so much in the monotonous formula "a child is being beaten" can probably be interpreted in a special way. The child which is being beaten (or caressed) may ultimately be nothing more nor less than the clitoris itself, so that at its very lowest level the statement will contain a confession of masturbation, which has remained attached to the content of the formula from its beginning in the phallic phase till later life.

A third consequence of penis-envy seems to be a loosening of the girl's relation with her mother as a love-object. The situation as a whole is not clear, but it can be seen that in the end the girl's mother, who sent her into the world so insufficiently equipped, is almost always held responsible for her lack of a penis. The way in which this comes about historically is often that soon after the girl has discovered that her genitals are unsatisfactory she begins to show jealousy of another child on the ground that her mother is fonder of it than of her, which serves as a reason for her giving up her affectionate relation to her mother. It will fit in with this if the child which has been preferred by her mother is made into the first object of the beating-phantasy which ends in masturbation. . . .

So far there has been no question of the Oedipus complex, nor has it up to this point played any part. But now the girl's libido slips into a new position along the line—there is no other way of putting it—of the equation "penis-child." She gives up her wish for a penis and puts in place of it a wish for a child: and *with that purpose in view* she takes her father as a love-object. Her mother becomes the object of her jealousy. The girl has turned into a little woman. If I am to credit a single analytic instance, this new situation can give rise to physical sensations which would have to be regarded as a premature awakening of the female genital apparatus. When the girl's attachment to her father comes to grief later on and has to be abandoned, it may give place to an identification with him and the girl may thus return to her masculinity complex and perhaps remain fixated in it.

Notes upon a Case
of Obsessional Neurosis

The following excerpts from a case history of obsessional neurosis illustrate Freud's theories of the causes of neurosis and provide a glimpse of the techniques he used with patients.

EXTRACTS FROM THE CASE HISTORY

A youngish man of university education introduced himself to me with the statement that he had suffered from obsessions ever since his childhood but with particular intensity for the last four years. The chief features of his disorder were *fears* that something might happen to two people of whom he was very fond—his father and a lady whom he admired. Besides this he was aware of *compulsive impulses*—such as an impulse, for instance, to cut his throat with a razor; and further he produced *prohibitions*, sometimes in connection with quite unimportant things. He had wasted years, he told me, in fighting against these ideas of his, and in this way had lost much ground in the course of his life. He had tried various treatments, but none had been of any use to him except a course of hydrotherapy at a sanatorium near ——; and this, he thought, had probably only been because he had made an acquaintance there which had led to regular sexual intercourse. Here he had no opportunities of the sort, and he seldom had intercourse and only at irregular intervals. He felt disgust at prostitutes. Altogether, he said, his sexual life had been stunted; onanism had played only a small part in it, in his sixteenth or seventeenth year. His potency was normal; he had first performed coitus at the age of twenty-six.

He gave me the impression of being a clear-headed and shrewd person. When I asked him what it was that made him lay such stress upon telling me about his sex-

The excerpts in this section are taken from Sigmund Freud's *Notes upon a Case of Obsessional Neurosis*, in *Collected Papers*, Vol. 3, edited by Ernest Jones, authorized translation by Alix Strachey and James Strachey (London: Hogarth Press and Institute of Psycho-Analysis, 1956), pp. 296–355, by arrangement with Paterson Marsh Ltd., London.

ual life, he replied that that was what he knew about my theories. Actually, however, he had read none of my writings, except that a short time before he had been turning over the pages of one of my books and had come across the explanation of some curious verbal associations[1] which had so much reminded him of some of his own "efforts of thought" in connection with his ideas that he had decided to put himself in my hands.

(a) THE BEGINNING OF THE TREATMENT

The next day I made him pledge himself to submit to the one and only condition of the treatment—namely, to say everything that came into his head, even if it was *unpleasant* to him, or seemed *unimportant or irrelevant* or *senseless*. I then gave him leave to start his communications with any subject he pleased, and he began as follows:[2]

He had a friend, he told me, of whom he had an extraordinarily high opinion. He used always to go to him when he was tormented by some criminal impulse, and ask him whether he despised him as a criminal. His friend used then to give him moral support by assuring him that he was a man of irreproachable conduct, and had probably been in the habit, from his youth onwards, of taking a dark view of his own life. At an earlier date, he went on, another person had exercised a similar influence over him. This was a nineteen-year-old student (he himself had been fourteen or fifteen at the time) who had taken a liking to him, and had raised his self-esteem to an extraordinary degree, so that he appeared to himself to be a genius. This student had subsequently become his tutor, and had suddenly altered his behaviour and begun treating him as though he were an idiot. At length he had noticed that the student was interested in one of his sisters, and had realized that he had only taken him up in order to gain admission into the house. This had been the first great blow of his life.

He then proceeded without any apparent transition:

(b) INFANTILE SEXUALITY

"My sexual life began very early. I can remember a scene out of my fourth or fifth year. (From my sixth year onwards I can remember everything.) This scene came into my head quite distinctly, years later. We had a very pretty young governess called Fräulein Peter.[3] One evening she was lying on the sofa lightly dressed, and reading. I was lying beside her, and begged her to let me creep under her skirt. She told me I might, so long as I said nothing to any one about it. She had very little on, and I fingered her genitals and the lower part of her body, which struck me as very queer. After this I was left with a burning and tormenting curiosity to see the female body. I can still remember the intense excitement with which I waited at the Baths (which I was still allowed to go to with the governess and my sisters) for the governess to undress and get into the water. I can remember more things from my sixth year onwards. At that time we had another governess, who was also young and good-looking. She had abscesses on her buttocks which she was in the habit of expressing at night. I used to wait eagerly for that moment, to appease my curiosity. It was just the same at the Baths—though Fräulein Lina was more reserved than her predecessor." (In reply to a question which I threw in, "As a rule," the patient told me, "I did not sleep in her room, but mostly with my parents.") "I remember a scene which must have taken place when I was seven years old.[4] We were sitting together one evening—the governess, the cook, another servant-girl, myself and my brother, who was eighteen months younger than me. The young women were talking, and I suddenly became aware of Fräulein Lina saying: 'It could be done with the little one; but Paul' (that was I) 'is too clumsy, he would be sure to miss it.' I did not understand clearly what was meant, but I felt the slight and began to cry. Lina comforted me, and told me how a girl, who had done something of the kind with a little boy she was in charge of, had been put in prison for several months. I do not believe she actually did anything wrong with me, but I took a great many liberties with her. When I got to her bed I used to uncover her and touch her, and she made no objections. She was not very intelligent, and clearly had very strong sexual cravings. At twenty-three she had already had a child. She afterwards married its father, so that to-day she is a Frau Hofrat.[5] Even now I often see her in the street.

"When I was six years old I already suffered from erections, and I know that once I went to my mother to complain about them. I know too that in doing so I had some misgivings to get over, for I had the feeling that there was some connection between this subject and my ideas and inquisitiveness, and at that time I used to have a morbid idea *that my parents knew my thoughts; I explained this to myself by supposing that I had spoken them out loud, without having heard myself do it.* I look on this as the beginning of my illness. There were certain people, girls, who pleased me very much, and I had a very strong wish *to see them naked.* But in wishing this I had *an uncanny feeling, as though something must happen if I though such things, and as though I must do all sorts of things to prevent it.*"

(In reply to a question he gave an example of these fears: "For instance, *that my father might die.*") "Thoughts about my father's death occupied my mind from a very early age and for a long period of time, and greatly depressed me."

At this point I learnt with astonishment that the patient's father, with whom his obsessional fears were still occupied at that actual time, had died several years previously. . . .

(c) THE GREAT OBSESSIVE FEAR

"I think I shall begin to-day with the experience which was the direct occasion of my coming to you. It was in August during the manoeuvers at ——. I had been suffering before, and tormenting myself with all kinds of obsessional thoughts, but they had quickly passed off during the manoeuvers. I was keen to show regular officers that people like me had not only learnt a good deal but could stand a good deal too. One day we started from —— on a short march. During a halt I lost my pince-nez [eyeglasses], and, although I could easily have found them, I did not want to delay our start, so I gave them up. But I wired to my opticians in Vienna to send me another pair by the next post. During that same halt I sat between two officers, one of whom, a captain with a Czech name, was to be of no small importance to me. I had a kind of dread of him, *for he was obviously fond of cruelty.* I do not say he was a bad man, but at the officers' mess he had repeatedly defended the introduction of corporal punishment, so that I had been obliged to disagree with him very sharply. Well, during this halt we got into conversation, and the captain told me he had read of a specially horrible punishment used in the East . . . "

Here the patient broke off, got up from the sofa, and begged me to spare him the recital of the details. I assured him that I myself had no taste whatever for cruelty, and certainly had no desire to torment him, but that naturally I could not grant him something which was beyond my power. He might just as well ask me to give him the moon. The overcoming of resistances was a law of the treatment, and on no consideration could it be dispensed with. (I had explained the idea of "resistance" to him at the beginning of the hour, when he told me there was much in himself which he would have to overcome if he was to relate this experience of his.) I went on to say that I would do all I could, nevertheless, to guess the full meaning of any hints he gave me. Was he perhaps thinking of impalement?— "No, not that; . . . the criminal was tied up . . ."—he expressed himself so indistinctly that I could not immediately guess in what position—" . . . a pot was turned upside down on his buttocks . . . some *rats* were put into it . . . and they . . ."—he had again got up, and was showing every sign of horror and resistance—" . . . *bored their way in* . . ." —Into his anus, I helped him out.

At all the more important moments while he was telling his story his face took on a very strange, composite expression. I could only interpret it as one of *horror at pleasure of his own of which he himself was unaware.* He proceeded with the greatest difficulty: "At that moment the idea flashed through my mind *that this was happening to a person who was very dear to me.*"[6] In answer to a direct question he said that it was not he himself who was carrying out the punishment, but that it was being carried out as it were impersonally. After a little prompting I learnt that the person to whom this "idea" of his related was the lady whom he admired.

He broke off his story in order to assure me that these thoughts were entirely foreign and repugnant to him, and to tell me that everything which had followed in their train had passed through his mind with the most extraordinary rapidity. Simultaneously with the idea there always appeared a "sanction," that is to say, the defensive measure which he was obliged to adopt in order to prevent the phantasy from being fulfilled. When the captain had spoken of this ghastly punishment, he went on, and these ideas had come into his head, by employing his usual formulas (a "But" accompanied by a gesture of repudiation, and the phrase "Whatever are you thinking of ?") he had just succeeded in warding off *both* of them.

This "both" took me aback, and it has no doubt also mystified the reader. For so far we have heard only of one idea—of the rat punishment being carried out upon the lady. He was now obliged to admit that a second idea had occurred to him simultaneously, namely, the idea of the punishment also being applied to his father. As his father had died many years previously, this obsessive fear was much more nonsensical even than the first, and accordingly it had attempted to escape being confessed to for a little while longer.

That evening, he continued, the same captain had handed him a packet that had arrived by the post and had said: "Lieutenant A. has paid the charges for you. You must pay him back." The packet had contained the pince-nez that he had wired for. At that instant, however, a "sanction" had taken shape in his mind, namely, *that he was not to pay back the money* or it would happen—(that is, the phantasy about the rats would come true as regards his father and the lady). And immediately, in accordance with a type of procedure with which he was familiar, to combat this sanction there had arisen a command in the shape of a vow: *"You must pay back the 3.80 crowns to Lieutenant A."* He had said these words to himself almost half aloud.

Two days later the manoeuvres had come to an end. He had spent the whole of the intervening time in efforts at repaying Lieutenant A. the small amount in question; but a succession of difficulties of an apparently *external* nature had arisen to prevent it. First he had tried to effect the payment through another officer who had been going to the post office. But he had been much relieved when this officer brought him back the money, saying that he had not met Lieutenant A. there, for this method of fulfilling his vow had not satisfied him, as it did not correspond with the wording, which ran: "You must pay back the money to Lieutenant A." Finally, he had met Lieutenant A., the person he was looking for; but he had refused to accept the money, declaring that he had not paid anything for him, and had nothing whatever to do with the post, which was the business of Lieutenant B. This had thrown my patient into great perplexity, for it meant that he was unable to keep his vow, since it had been based upon false premises. He had excogitated a very curious means of getting out of his difficulty, namely, that he should go to the post office with both the men, A. and B., that A. should give the young lady there the 3.80 crowns, that the young lady should give them to B., and that then he himself should pay back the 3.80 crowns to A. according to the wording of his vow. . . .

Students:

1. Identify the Freudian concepts and techniques which seem most evident from the pages you just read.
2. What, so far, strikes you as significant regarding this case?

The case at hand presents a polite, thoroughly civil lawyer whose thoughts render him unable to work. How long do you think the treatment will be? Why? A number of curious things are recounted; the patient, though in his late twenties, often focused on his father, who had died years before, and Freud appears to leave the course of treatment to the patient. Perhaps the most curious element is the surfacing of troubling thoughts and emotions long after the events associated with them. Drawing on your knowledge of psychoanalytic theory, do you view the specific triggering event of the patient's obsessive thoughts/emotions as the origin (cause) of his illness?

(*d*) INITIATION INTO THE NATURE OF THE TREATMENT

The reader must not expect to hear at once what light I have to throw upon the patient's strange and senseless obsessions about the rats. The true technique of psychoanalysis requires the physician to suppress his curiosity and leaves the patient complete freedom in choosing the order in which topics shall succeed each other during the treatment. At the fourth sitting, accordingly, I received the patient with the question: "And how do you intend to proceed to-day?"

"I have decided to tell you something which I consider most important and which has tormented me from the very first." He then told me at great length the story of the last illness of his father, who had died of emphysema nine years previously. One evening, thinking that the condition was one which would come to a crisis, he had asked the doctor when the danger could be regarded as over. "The evening of the day after to-morrow," had been the reply. It had never entered his head that his father might not survive that limit. At half-past eleven at night he had lain down for an hour's rest. He had woken up at one o'clock, and had been told by a medical friend that his father had died. He had reproached himself with not having been present at his death; and the reproach had been intensified when the nurse told him that his father had spoken his name once during the last days, and had said to her as she came up to the bed: "Is that Paul?" He had thought he noticed that his mother and sisters had been inclined to reproach themselves in a similar way; but they had never spoken about it. At first, however, the reproach had not tormented him. For a long time he had not realized the fact of his father's death. It had constantly happened that when he heard a good joke, he would say to himself: "I must tell Father that." His imagination, too, had been occupied with his father, so that often, when there was a knock at the door, he would think: "Here comes Father," and when he walked into a room he would expect to find his father in it. And although he had never forgotten that his father was dead, the prospect of seeing a ghostly apparition of this kind had had no terrors for him; on the contrary, he had greatly desired it. It had not been until eighteen months later that the recollection of his neglect had recurred to him and begun to torment him terribly, so that he had come to treat himself as a criminal. The occasion of this happening had been the death of an aunt by marriage and of a visit of condolence that he had paid at her house. From that time forward he had extended the structure of his obsessional thoughts so as to include the next world. The immediate consequence of this development had been that he became seriously incapacitated from working.[7] He told me that the only thing that had kept him going at that time had been the consolation given him by his friend, who had always brushed his self-reproaches aside on the ground that they were grossly exaggerated. Hearing this, I took the opportunity of giving him a first glance at the underlying principles of psycho-analytic therapy. When there is a *mésalliance*,[8] I began, between an affect and its ideational content (in this instance, between the intensity of the self-reproach and the occasion for it), a layman will say that the affect is too great for the occasion—that it is exaggerated—and that consequently the inference following from the self-reproach (the inference, that is, that the patient is a criminal) is false. On the contrary, the physician says: "No. The affect is justified. The sense of guilt cannot in itself be further criticized. But it belongs to another content, which is unknown (*unconscious*), and which requires to be looked for. The known ideational content has only got into its actual position owing to a mistaken association. We are not used to feeling strong affects without their having any ideational content, and therefore, if the content is missing, we seize as a substitute upon another content which is in some way or other suitable, much as our police, when they cannot catch the right murderer, arrest a wrong one instead. Moreover, this fact of there being a mistaken association is the only way of accounting for the powerlessness of logical processes in combating the tormenting idea. I concluded by admitting that this new way of looking at the matter gave immediate rise to some hard problems; for how could he admit that his self-reproach of being a criminal towards his father was justified, when he must know that as a matter of fact he had never committed any crime against him?

At the next sitting the patient showed great interest in what I had said, but ventured, so he told me, to bring forward a few doubts.— How, he asked, could the information that the self-reproach, the sense of guilt, was justified have a therapeutic effect?— I explained that it was not the information that had this effect, but the discovery of the unknown content to which the self-reproach was really attached.— Yes, he said, that was the precise point to which his question had been directed.— I then made some short observations upon *the psychological differences between the conscious and the unconscious*, and upon the fact that everything conscious was subject to a process of wearing-away, while what was unconscious was relatively unchangeable; and I illustrated my remarks by pointing to the antiques standing about in my room. They were, in fact, I said, only objects found in a tomb, and their burial had been their preservation: the destruction of Pompeii was only beginning now that it had been dug up.— Was there any guarantee, he next inquired, of what one's attitude would be towards what was discovered? One man, he thought, would no doubt behave in such a way as to get the better of his self-reproach, but another would not.— No, I said, it followed from the nature of the circumstances that in every case the affect would for the most part be overcome during the progress of the work itself. Every effort was made to preserve Pompeii, whereas people were anxious to be rid of tormenting ideas like his.— He had said to himself, he went on, that a self-reproach could only arise from a breach of a person's own inner moral principles and not from that of any external ones.— I agreed, and said that the man who merely breaks an external law often regards himself as a hero. Such an occurrence, he continued, was thus only possible where a *disintegration of the personality* was already present. Was there a possibility of his effecting a re-integration of his personality? If this could be done, he thought he would be able to make a success of his life, perhaps a better one than most people.— I replied that I was in complete agreement with this notion of a splitting of his personality. He had only to assimilate this new contrast, between a moral self and an evil one, with the contrast I had already mentioned, between the conscious and the unconscious. The moral self was the conscious, the evil self was the unconscious.[9]— He then said that, though he considered himself a moral person, he could quite definitely remember having done things in his *childhood* which came from his other self.— I remarked that here he had incidentally hit upon one of the chief characteristics of the unconscious, namely, its relation to the *infantile*. The unconscious, I explained, *was* the infantile; it was that part of the self which had become separated off from it in infancy, which had not shared the later stages of its development, and which had in consequence become *repressed*. It was the derivatives of this repressed unconscious that were responsible for the involuntary thoughts which constituted his illness. He might now, I added, discover yet another characteristic of the unconscious; it was a discovery which I should be glad to let him make for himself.— He found nothing more to say in this immediate connection, but instead he expressed a doubt whether it was possible to undo modifications of such long standing. What, in particular, could be done against his idea about the next world, for it could not be refuted by logic?— I told him I did not dispute the gravity of his case nor the significance of his pathological constructions; but at the same time his youth was very much in his favour as well as the intactness of his personality. In this connection I said a word or two upon the good opinion I had formed of him, and this gave him visible pleasure.

> The following passage drives us further into the patient's mental world, and we view psychoanalytic theory put to practice. Freud encounters resistance and perplexity from the patient regarding Freud's focus on the patient's repressed wish for his father's death. However, additional events containing thoughts for the death of the patient's father are revealed. While most patients may well be alarmed by Freud's focus, he reminds the patient that *he* has brought up his childhood sexual events and his father's real or perceived role. We are reminded here of Freud's disbelief in random thoughts and events; all thoughts and events fit an often unknown, larger, logical pattern.

At the next sitting he began by saying that he must tell me an event in his childhood. From the age of seven, as he had already told me, he had had a fear that his parents guessed his thoughts, and this fear had in fact persisted all through his life. When he was twelve years old he had been in love with a little girl, the sister of a friend of his. (In answer to a question he said that his love had not been sensual; he had not wanted to see her naked for she was too small.) But she had not shown him as much affection as he had desired. And thereupon the idea had come to him that she would be kind to him if some misfortune were to befall him; and as an instance of such a misfortune his father's death had forced itself upon his mind. He had at once rejected the idea with energy. And even now he could not admit the possibility that what had arisen in this way could have been a "wish"; it had clearly been no more than a "connection of thought."[10]— By way of objection I asked him why, if it had not been a wish, he had repudiated it.— Merely, he replied, on account of the content of the idea, the notion that his father might die.— I remarked that he was treating the phrase as though it were one that involved *lèse-majesté*;[11] it was well known, of course, that it was equally punishable to say "The Emperor is an ass" or to disguise the forbidden words by saying "If any one says, etc., . . . then he will have me to reckon with." I added that I could easily insert the idea which he had so energetically repudiated into a context which would exclude the possibility of any such repudiation: for instance, "If my father dies, I shall kill myself upon his grave."— He was shaken, but did not abandon his objection. I therefore broke off the argument with the remark that I felt sure this had not been the first occurrence of his idea of his father's dying; it had evidently originated at an earlier date, and some day we should have to trace back its history.— He then proceeded to tell me that a precisely similar thought had flashed through his mind a second time, six months before his father's death.[12] At that time he had already been in love with his lady, but financial obstacles made it impossible to think of an alliance with her. The idea had then occurred to him that *his father's death might make him rich enough to marry her.* In defending himself against this idea he had gone to the length of wishing that his father might leave him nothing at all, so that he might have no compensation for his terrible loss. The same idea, though in a much milder form, had come to him for a third time, on the day before his father's death. He had then thought: "Now I may be going to lose what I love most"; and then had come the contradiction: "No, there is some one else whose loss would be even more painful to you."[13] These thoughts surprised him very much, for he was quite certain that his father's death could never have been an object of his desire but only of his fear.— After his forcible enunciation of these words I thought it advisable to bring a fresh piece of theory to his notice. According to psycho-analytical theory, I told him, every fear corresponded to a former wish which was now repressed; we were therefore obliged to believe the exact contrary of what he had asserted. This would also fit in with another theoretical requirement, namely, that the unconscious must be the precise contrary of the conscious.— He was much agitated at this and very incredulous. He wondered how he could possibly have had such a wish, considering that he loved his father more than any one else in the world; there could be no doubt that he would have renounced all his own prospects of happiness if by so doing he could have saved his father's life.— I answered that it was precisely such intense love as his that was the condition of the repressed hatred. In the case of people to whom he felt indifferent he would certainly have no difficulty in maintaining side by side inclinations to a moderate liking and to an equally moderate dislike: supposing, for instance, that he were an official, he might think that his chief was agreeable as a superior, but at the same time pettifogging as a lawyer and inhuman as a judge. Shakespeare makes Brutus speak in a similar way of Julius Caesar: "As Caesar loved me, I weep for him; as he was fortunate, I rejoice at it; as he was valiant, I honour him; but as he was ambitious, I slew him." But these words already strike us as rather strange, and for the very reason that we had imagined Brutus's feeling for Caesar as something deeper. In the case of some one who was closer to him, of his for instance, he would wish his feelings to be unmixed, and consequently, as was only human, he would overlook her faults, since they might make him dislike her—he would ignore them as though he were blind to them. So it was precisely the intensity of his love that would not allow his hatred—though to give it such a name was to caricature the feeling—to remain conscious. To be sure, the hatred must have a source, and to discover that source was certainly a problem; his own statements pointed to the time when he was afraid that his parents guessed his thoughts. On the other hand, too, it might be asked why this intense love of his had not succeeded in extinguishing his hatred, as usually happened where there were two opposing impulses. We could only presume that the hatred must flow from some source, must be connected with some particular cause, which made it indestructible. On the one hand, then, some connection of this sort must be keeping his hatred for his father alive, while on the other hand, his intense love prevented it from becoming conscious. Therefore nothing remained for it but to exist in the unconscious, though it was able from time to time to flash out for a moment into consciousness.

He admitted that all of this sounded quite plausible, but he was naturally not in the very least convinced by it.[14] He would venture to ask, he said, how it was that an idea of this kind could have remissions, how it could appear for a moment when he was twelve years old, and again when he was twenty, and then once more two years later, this time for good. He could not believe that his hostility had been extinguished in the intervals, and yet during them there had been no sign of self-reproaches.— To this I replied that whenever any one asked a question like that, he was already prepared with an answer; he needed only to be encouraged to go on talking.— He then proceeded, somewhat disconnectedly as it seemed, to say that he had been his father's best friend, and that his father had been his. Except on a few subjects, upon which fathers and sons usually hold aloof from one another—(What could he mean by that?)—there had been a greater intimacy between them than there now was between him and his best friend. As regards the lady on whose account he had slighted his father in that idea of his, it was true that he had loved her very much, but he had never felt really sensual wishes towards her, such as he had constantly had in his childhood. Altogether, in his childhood his sensual impulses had been much stronger than during his puberty.— At this I told him I thought he had now produced the answer we were waiting for, and had at the same time discovered the third great characteristic of the unconscious. The source from which his hostility to his father derived its indestructibility was evidently something in the nature of *sensual desires*, and in that connection he must have felt his father as in some way or other an *interference*. A conflict of this kind, I added, between sensuality and childish love was entirely typical. The remissions he had spoken of had occurred because the premature explosion of his sensual feelings had had as its immediate consequence a considerable diminution of their violence. It was not until he was once more seized with intense erotic desires that his hostility reappeared again owing to the revival of the old situation. I then got him to agree that I had not led him on to the subject either of childhood or of sex, but that he had raised them both of his own free will.— He then went on to ask why he had not simply come to a decision, at the time he was in love with the lady, that his father's interference with that love could not for a moment weigh against his love of his father.— I replied that it was scarcely possible to destroy a person *in absentia*. Such a decision would only have been possible if the wish that he took objection to had made its first appearance on that occasion; whereas, as a matter of fact, it was *a long-repressed wish*, towards which he could not behave otherwise than he had formerly done, and which was consequently immune from destruction. This wish (to get rid of his father as being an interference) must have originated at a time when circumstances had been very different—at a time, perhaps, when he had not loved his father more than the person whom he desired sensually, or when he was incapable of making a clear decision. It must have been in his very early childhood, therefore, before he had reached the age of six, and before the date at which his memory became continuous; and things must have remained in the same state ever since.— With this piece of construction our discussion was broken off for the time being.

At the next sitting, which was the seventh, he took up the same subject once more. He could not believe, he said, that he had ever entertained such a wish against his father. He remembered a story of Sudermann's, he went on, that had made a deep impression upon him. In this story there was a woman who, as she sat by her sister's sickbed, felt a wish that her sister should die so that she herself might marry her husband. The woman thereupon committed suicide, thinking she was not fit to live after being guilty of such baseness. He could understand this, he said, and it would be only right if his thoughts were the death of him, for he deserved nothing less.[15]— I remarked that it was well known to us that patients derived a certain satisfaction from their sufferings, so that in reality they all resisted their own recovery to some extent. He must never lose sight of the fact that a treatment like ours proceeded to the accompaniment of a *constant resistance;* I should be repeatedly reminding him of this fact.

He then went on to say that he would like to speak of a criminal act, in the author of which he did not recognize himself, though he quite clearly recollected doing it. He quoted a saying of Nietzsche's: "'I did this,' says my Memory. 'I cannot have done this,' says my Pride and remains inexorable. In the end—Memory yields." "Well," he continued, "my memory has *not* yielded on this point."— "That is because you derive pleasure from your reproaches as being a means of self-punishment."— "My younger brother—I am really very fond of him now, and he is causing me a great deal of worry just at present, for he wants to make what I consider a preposterous match; I have thought before now of going and killing the person so as to prevent his marrying her—well, my younger brother and I used to fight a lot when we were children. We were very fond of one another at the same time, and were inseparable; but I was plainly filled with jealousy, as he was the stronger and better-looking of the two and consequently the favourite."— "Yes. You have already given me a description of a scene of jealousy in connection with Fräulein Lina."— "Very well then, on some such occasion (it was certainly before I was eight years old, for I was not going to school yet, which I began to do when I was eight)—on some such occasion, this is what I did. We both had toy guns of the usual make. I loaded mine with the ramrod and told him that if he looked up the barrel he would see something. Then, while he was looking in, I pulled the trigger. He was hit on the forehead and not hurt; but I had meant to hurt him very much indeed. Afterwards I was quite beside myself, and threw myself on the ground and asked myself how ever I could have done such a thing. But I *did* do it."— I took the opportunity of urging my case. If he had preserved the recollection of an action so foreign to him as this, he could not, I maintained, deny the possibility of something similar, which he had now forgotten entirely, having happened at a still earlier age in relation to his father.— He then told me he was aware of having felt other vindictive impulses, this time towards the lady he admired so much, of whose character he painted a glowing picture. It might be true, he said, that she could not love easily; but she was reserving her whole self for the one man to whom she would some day belong. She did not love him. When he had become certain of that, a conscious phantasy had taken shape in his mind of how he should grow very rich and marry some one else, and should then take her to call on the lady in order to hurt her feelings. But at that point the phantasy had broken down, for he had been obliged to own to himself that the other woman, his wife, was completely indifferent to him; then his thoughts had become confused, till finally it had been clearly borne in upon him that this other woman would have to die. In this phantasy, just as in his attempt upon his brother, he recognized the quality of *cowardice* which was so particularly horrible to him.— In the further course of our conversation I pointed out to him that he ought logically to consider himself as in no way responsible for any of these traits in his character; for all of these reprehensible impulses originated from his infancy, and were only derivatives of his infantile character surviving in his unconscious; and he must know that moral responsibility could not be applied to children. It was only by a process of development, I added, that a man, with his moral responsibility, grew up out of the sum of his infantile predispositions.[16] He expressed a doubt, however, whether all his evil impulses had originated from that source. But I promised to prove it to him in the course of the treatment.

He went on to adduce the fact of his illness having become so enormously intensified since his father's death; and I said I agreed with him in so far as I regarded his sorrow at his father's death as the chief source of the *intensity* of his illness. His sorrow had found, as it were, a pathological expression in his illness, Whereas, I told him, a normal period of mourning would last from one to two years, a pathological one like his would last indefinitely.

This is as much of the present case history as I am able to report in a detailed and consecutive manner. It coincides roughly with the expository portion of the treatment; this lasted in all for more than eleven months.

> The following excerpt contains moments where the analysand (patient), perhaps unknowingly, encourages the analyst's suspicion of childhood events which resulted in the patient's ambivalence toward his father. Again, we witness the analysand's resistance to owning or admitting to negative feelings for his father, while he continues to recall events and statements indicating otherwise. Also, many of the patient's curious thoughts or statements involve his father, his father's death, and a woman.
>
> *Students:*
> What do you think is the relationship between the analysand's obsessional thoughts and his feelings toward his father?

But I must now return to a more detailed examination of the exciting cause of our patient's illness. His mother had been brought up in a wealthy family with which she was distantly connected. This family carried on a large industrial concern. His father, at the time of his marriage, had been taken into the business, and had thus by his marriage made himself a fairly comfortable position. The patient had learnt from some chaff exchanged between his parents (whose marriage was an extremely happy one) that his father, some time before making his mother's acquaintance, had made advances to a pretty but penniless girl of humble birth. So much by way of introduction. After his father's death the patient's mother told him one day that she had been discussing his future with her rich relations, and that one of her cousins had declared himself ready to let him marry one of his daughters when his education was completed; a business connection with the firm would offer him a brilliant opening in his profession. This family plan stirred up in him a conflict as to whether he should remain faithful to the lady he loved in spite of her poverty, or whether he should follow in his father's footsteps and marry the lovely, rich, and well-connected girl who had been assigned to him. And he resolved this conflict, which was in fact one between his love and the persisting influence of his father's wishes, by falling ill; or, to put it more correctly, by falling ill he avoided the task of resolving it in real life.[17]

The proof that this view was correct lies in the fact that the chief result of his illness was an obstinate incapacity for work, which allowed him to postpone the completion of his education for years. But the results of such an illness are never unintentional; what appears to be the consequence of the illness is in reality the cause or motive of falling ill.

As was to be expected, the patient did not, to begin with, accept my elucidation of the matter. He could not imagine, he said, that the plan of marriage could have had any such effects: it had not made the slightest impression on him at the time. But in the further course of treatment he was forcibly brought to believe in the truth of my suspicion, and in a most singular manner. With the help of a transference phantasy, he experienced, as though it were new and belonged to the present, the very episode from the past which he had forgotten, or which had only passed through his mind unconsciously. There came an obscure and difficult period in the treatment; eventually it turned out that he had once met a young girl on the stairs in my house and had on the spot promoted her into being my daughter. She had pleased him, and he pictured to himself that the only reason I was so kind and incredibly patient with him was that I wanted to have him for a son-in-law. At the same time he raised the wealth and position of my family to a level which agreed with the model he had in mind. But his undying love for his lady fought against the temptation. After we had gone through a series of the severest resistances and bitterest vituperations on his part, he could no longer remain blind to the overwhelming effect of the perfect analogy between the transference phantasy and the actual state of affairs in the past. . . .

(g) THE FATHER COMPLEX AND THE SOLUTION OF THE RAT IDEA

From the exciting cause of the patient's illness in his adult years there was a thread leading back to his childhood. He had found himself in a situation similar to that in which, as he knew or suspected, his father had been before *his* marriage; and he had thus been able to identify himself with his father. But his dead father was involved in his recent attack in yet another way. The conflict at the root of his illness was in essentials a struggle between the persisting influence of his father's wishes and his own amatory predilections. If we take into consideration what the patient reported in the course of the first hours of his treatment, we shall not be able to avoid a suspicion that this struggle was a very ancient one and had arisen as far back as in his childhood.

By all accounts our patient's father was a most excellent man. Before his marriage he had been a non-commissioned officer, and, as relics of that period of his life, he had retained a straightforward soldierly manner and a *penchant* for using downright language. Apart from those virtues which are celebrated upon every tombstone, he was distinguished by a hearty sense of humour and a kindly tolerance towards his fellow-men. That he could be hasty and violent was certainly not inconsistent with his other qualities, but was rather a necessary complement to them; but it occasionally brought down the most severe castigations upon the children, while they were young and naughty. When they grew up, however, he differed from other fathers in not attempting to exalt himself into a sacrosanct authority, but in sharing with them a knowledge of the little failures and misfortunes of his life with good-natured candour. His son was certainly not exaggerating when he declared that they had lived together like the best of friends, except upon a single point. And it must no doubt have been in connection with that very point that thoughts about his father's death had occupied his mind when he was a small boy with unusual and undue intensity, and that those thoughts made their appearance in the wording of the obsessional ideas of his childhood; and it can only have been in that same connection that he was able to wish for his father's death, in order that a certain little girl's sympathy might be aroused and that she might become kinder towards him.

There can be no question that there was something in the sphere of sexuality that stood between the father and son, and that the father had come into some sort of opposition to the son's prematurely developed erotic life. Several years after his father's death, the first time he experienced the pleasurable sensations of copulation, an idea sprang into his mind: "This is glorious! One might murder one's father for this!" This was at once an echo and an elucidation of the obsessional ideas of his childhood. Moreover, his father, shortly before his death, had directly opposed what later became our patient's dominating passion. He had noticed that his son was always in the lady's company, and had advised him to keep away from her, saying that it was imprudent of him and that he would only make a fool of himself.

To this unimpeachable body of evidence we shall be able to add fresh material, if we turn to the history of the onanistic side of our patient's sexual activities. There is a conflict between the opinions of doctors and patients on this subject which has not hitherto been properly appreciated. The patients are unanimous in their belief that onanism, by which they mean masturbation during puberty, is the root and origin of all their troubles. The doctors are, upon the whole, unable to decide what line to take; but, influenced by the knowledge that not only neurotics but most normal persons pass through a period of onanism during their puberty, the majority of them are inclined to dismiss the patient's assertions as gross exaggerations. In my opinion the patients are once again nearer to a correct view than the doctors; for the patients have some glimmering notion of the truth, while the doctors are in danger of overlooking an essential point. The thesis propounded by the patients certainly does not correspond to the facts in the sense in which they themselves construe it, namely, that onanism during puberty (which may almost be described as a typical occurrence) is responsible for all neurotic disturbances. Their thesis requires interpretation. The onanism of puberty is in fact no more than a revival of the onanism of infancy, a subject which has hitherto invariably been neglected. Infantile onanism reaches a kind of climax, as a rule, between the ages of three and four or five; and it is the clearest expression of a child's sexual constitution, in which the aetiology of subsequent neuroses must be sought. In this disguised way, therefore, the patients are putting the blame for their illnesses upon their infantile sexuality; and they are perfectly right in doing so. On the other hand, the problem of onanism becomes insoluble if we attempt to treat it as a clinical unit, and forget that it can represent the discharge of every variety of sexual component and of every sort of phantasy to which such components can give rise. The injurious effects of onanism are only in a very small degree autonomous—that is to say, determined by its own nature. They are in substance merely part and parcel of the pathogenic significance of the sexual life as a whole. The fact that so many people can tolerate onanism—that is, a certain amount of it—without injury merely shows that their sexual constitution and the course of development of their sexual life have been such as to allow them to exercise the sexual function within the limits of what is culturally permissible;[18] whereas other people, because their sexual constitution has been less favourable or their development has been disturbed, fall ill as a result of their sexuality,—they cannot, that is, achieve the necessary suppression or sublimation of their sexual components without having recourse to inhibitions or substitute-formations.

Our present patient's behaviour in the matter of onanism was most remarkable. He did not indulge in it during puberty to any extent worth mentioning, and therefore, according to one set of views, he might have expected to be exempt from neurosis. On the other hand, an impulsion towards onanistic practices came over him in his twenty-first year, *shortly after his father's death.* He felt very much ashamed of himself each time he gave way to this kind of gratification, and soon foreswore the habit. From that time onwards it reappeared only upon rare and extraordinary occasions. It was provoked, he told me, when he experienced especially fine moments, or when he read especially fine passages. It occurred once, for instance, on a lovely summer's afternoon when, in the middle of Vienna, he heard a postilion blowing his horn in the most wonderful way, until a policeman stopped him, because blowing horns is not allowed in the centre of the town. And another time it happened when he read in *Dichtumg und Wahrheit* how the young Goethe had freed himself in a burst of tenderness from the effects of a curse which a jealous mistress had pronounced upon the next woman who should kiss his lips after her; he had long, almost superstitiously, suffered the curse to hold him back, but now he broke his bonds and kissed his love joyfully again and again.

It seemed to the patient not a little strange that he should be impelled to masturbate precisely upon such beautiful and uplifting occasions as these. But I could not help pointing out that these two occasions had something in common—a prohibition, and the defiance of a command.

We must also consider in the same connection his curious behaviour at a time when he was working for an examination and toying with his favourite phantasy that his father was still alive and might at any moment reappear. He used to arrange that his working hours should be as late as possible in the night. Between twelve and one o'clock at night he would interrupt his work, and open the front door of the flat as though his father were standing outside it; then, coming back into the hall, he would take out his penis and look at it in the looking-glass. This crazy conduct becomes intelligible if we suppose that he was acting as though he expected a visit from his father at the hour when ghosts are abroad. He had on the whole been idle at his work during his father's lifetime, and this had often been a cause of annoyance to his father. And now that he was returning as a ghost, he was to be delighted at finding his son hard at work. But it was impossible that his father should be delighted at the other part of his behaviour; in this therefore he must be defying him. Thus, in a single unintelligible obsessional act, he gave expression to the two sides of his relation with his father. . . .

Starting from these indications and from other data of a similar kind, I ventured to put forward a construction to the effect that when he was a child of under six he had been guilty of some sexual misdemeanour connected with onanism and had been soundly castigated for it by his father. This punishment, according to my hypothesis, had, it was true, put an end to his onanism, but on the other hand it had left behind it an ineradicable grudge against his father and had established him for all time in his role of an interferer with the patient's sexual enjoyment. To my great astonishment the patient then informed me that his mother had repeatedly described to him an occurrence of this kind which dated from his earliest childhood and had evidently escaped being forgotten by her on account of its remarkable consequences. He himself, however, had no recollection of it whatever. The tale was as follows. When he was very small—it became possible to establish the date more exactly owing to its having coincided with the fatal illness of an elder sister—he had done something naughty, for which his father had given him a beating. The little boy had flown into a terrible rage and had hurled abuse at his father even while he was under his blows. But as he knew no bad language, he had called him all the names of common objects that he could think of, and had screamed: "You lamp! You towel! You plate!" and so on. His father, shaken by such an outburst of elemental fury, had stopped beating him, and had declared: "The child will be either a great man or a great criminal!"[19] The patient believed that the scene made a permanent impression upon himself as well as upon his father. His father, he said, never beat him again; and he also attributed to this experience a part of the change which came over his own character. From that time forward he was a coward—out of fear of the violence of his own rage. His whole life long, moreover, he was terribly afraid of blows, and used to creep away and hide, filled with terror and indignation, when one of his brothers or sisters was beaten.

The patient subsequently questioned his mother again. She confirmed the story, adding that at the time he had been between three and four years old and that he had been given the punishment because be had *bitten* some one. She could remember no further details, except for a very uncertain idea that the person the little boy had hurt might have been his nurse. In her account there was no suggestion of his misdeed having been of a sexual nature.[20]

> This last passage will let you know if your interpretation of the case lines up with Freud's.

Let us, further, picture to ourselves the general conditions under which the formation of the patient's great obsessional idea occurred. His libido had been increased by a long period of abstinence coupled with the friendly welcome which a young officer can always reckon upon receiving when he goes among women. Moreover, at the time when he had started for the manoeuvers, there had been a certain coolness between himself and his lady. This intensification of his libido had inclined him to a renewal of his ancient struggle against his father's authority, and he had dared to think of having sexual intercourse with other women. His loyalty to his father's memory had grown weaker, his doubts as to his lady's merits had increased; and in that frame of mind he let himself be dragged into insulting the two of them, and had then punished himself for it. In doing so he had copied an old model. And when at the end of the manoeuvers he had hesitated so long whether he should travel to Vienna or whether he should stop and fulfil his vow,[21] he had represented in a single picture the two conflicts by which he had from the very first been torn—whether or no he should remain obedient to his father and whether or no he should remain faithful to his beloved.[22]

The Psychogenesis of a Case of Homosexuality in a Woman

The following case involves a young woman of eighteen whose parents want Freud to "cure" her of a strong infatuation for an older, disreputable woman. Despite the parents' views of homosexuality, Freud's perspective rests on his theories of infantile sexuality. What do you make of Freud's statement that the patient is not ill?

THE PSYCHOGENESIS OF A CASE OF HOMOSEXUALITY IN A WOMAN

Homosexuality in women, which is certainly not less common than in men, although much less glaring, has not only been ignored by the law, but has also been neglected by psycho-analytic research. The narration of a single case, not too pronounced in type, in which it was possible to trace its origin and development in the mind with complete certainty and almost without a gap may, therefore, have a certain claim to attention. If this presentation of it furnishes only the most general outlines of the various events concerned and of the conclusions reached from a study of the case, while suppressing all the characteristic details on which the interpretation is founded, this limitation is easily to be explained by the medical discretion necessary in discussing a recent case.

A beautiful and clever girl of eighteen, belonging to a family of good standing, had aroused displeasure and concern in her parents by the devoted adoration with which she pursued a certain "society lady" who was about ten years older than herself. The parents asserted that, in spite of her distinguished name, this lady was nothing but a *cocotte*. It was well known, they said, that she lived with a friend, a married woman, and had intimate relations with her, while at the same time she carried on promiscu-

The excerpts in this section are taken from Sigmund Freud's *The Psychogenesis of a Case of Homosexuality in a Woman*, edited and translated by James Strachey, in *Standard Edition of the Complete Psychological Works of Sigmund Freud*, Vol. 18 (London: Hogarth Press and Institute of Psycho-Analysis, 1955), pp. 147–172, by arrangement with Paterson Marsh Ltd., London.

ous affairs with a number of men. The girl did not contradict these evil reports, but neither did she allow them to interfere with her worship of the lady, although she herself was by no means lacking in a sense of decency and propriety. No prohibitions and no supervision hindered the girl from seizing every one of her rare opportunities of being together with her beloved, of ascertaining all her habits, of waiting for her for hours outside her door or at a tram-halt, of sending her gifts of flowers, and so on. It was evident that this one interest had swallowed up all others in the girl's mind. She did not trouble herself any further with educational studies, thought nothing of social functions or girlish pleasures, and kept up relations only with a few girl friends who could help her in the matter or serve as confidantes. The parents could not say to what lengths their daughter had gone in her relations with the questionable lady, whether the limits of devoted admiration had already been exceeded or not. They had never remarked in their daughter any interest in young men, nor pleasure in their attentions, while, on the other hand, they were sure that her present attachment to a woman was only a continuation, in a more marked degree, of a feeling she had displayed of recent years for other members of her own sex which had already aroused her father's suspicion and anger.

There were two details of her behaviour, in apparent contrast with each other, that most especially vexed her parents. On the one hand, she did not scruple to appear in the most frequented streets in the company of her undesirable friend, being thus quite neglectful of her own reputation; while, on the other hand, she disdained no means of deception, no excuses and no lies that would make meetings with her possible and cover them. She thus showed herself too open in one respect and full of deceitfulness in the other. One day it happened, indeed, as was sooner or later inevitable in the circumstances, that the father met his daughter in the company of the lady, about whom he had come to know. He passed them by with an angry glance which boded no good. Immediately afterwards the girl rushed off and flung herself over a wall down the side of a cutting on to the suburban railway line which ran close by. She paid for this undoubtedly serious attempt at suicide with a considerable time on her back in bed, though fortunately little permanent damage was done. After her recovery she found it easier to get her own way than before. The parents did not dare to oppose her with so much determination, and the lady, who up till then had received her advances coldly, was moved by such an unmistakable proof of serious passion and began to treat her in a more friendly manner.

About six months after this episode the parents sought medical advice and entrusted the physician with the task of bringing their daughter back to a normal state of mind. The girl's attempted suicide had evidently shown them that strong disciplinary measures at home were powerless to overcome her disorder. Before going further, however, it will be desirable to deal separately with the attitudes of her father and of her mother to the matter. The father was an earnest, worthy man, at bottom very tender-hearted, but he had to some extent estranged his children by the sternness he had adopted towards them. His treatment of his only daughter was too much influenced by consideration for his wife. When he first came to know of his daughter's homosexual tendencies he flew into a rage and tried to suppress them by threats. At that time perhaps he hesitated between different, though equally distressing, views—regarding her either as vicious, as degenerate, or as mentally afflicted. Even after the attempted suicide he did not achieve the lofty resignation shown by one of our medical colleagues who remarked of a similar irregularity in his own family: "Well, it's just a misfortune like any other." There was something about his daughter's homosexuality that aroused the deepest bitterness in him, and he was determined to combat it with all the means in his power. The low estimation in which psycho-analysis is so generally held in Vienna did not prevent him from turning to it for help. If this way failed he still had in reserve his strongest counter-measure: a speedy marriage was to awaken the natural instincts of the girl and stifle her unnatural tendencies.

The mother's attitude towards the girl was not so easy to grasp. She was still a youngish woman, who was evidently unwilling to give up her own claims to attractiveness. All that was clear was that she did not take her daughter's infatuation so tragically as did the father, nor was she so incensed at it. She had even for some time enjoyed her daughter's confidence concerning her passion. Her opposition to it seemed to have been aroused mainly by the harmful publicity with which the girl displayed her feelings. She had herself suffered for some years from neurotic troubles and enjoyed a great deal of consideration from her husband; she treated her children in quite different ways, being decidedly harsh towards her daughter and overindulgent to her three sons, the youngest of whom had been born after a long interval and was then not yet three years old. It was not easy to ascertain anything more definite about her character, for, owing to motives that will only later become intelligible, the patient was always reserved in what she said about her mother, whereas in regard to her father there was no question of this. . . .

Further unfavourable features in the present case were the facts that the girl was not in any way ill (she did not suffer from anything in herself, nor did she complain of her condition) and that the task to be carried out did not consist in resolving a neurotic conflict but in converting one variety of the genital organization of sexuality into the other. Such an achievement—the removal of genital inversion or homosexuality—is in my experience never an easy matter. On the contrary, I have found success possible only in specially favourable circumstances, and even then the success essentially consisted in making access to the opposite sex (which had hitherto been barred) possible to a person restricted to homosexuality, thus restoring his full bisexual functions. After that it lay with him to choose whether he wished to abandon the path that is banned by society, and in some cases he has done so. One must remember that normal sexuality too depends upon a restriction in the choice of object. In general, to undertake to convert a fully developed homosexual into a heterosexual does not offer much more prospect of success than the reverse, except that for good practical reasons the latter is never attempted.

The number of successes achieved by psycho-analytic treatment of the various forms of homosexuality, which incidentally are manifold, is indeed not very striking. As a rule the homosexual is not able to give up the object which provides him with pleasure, and one cannot convince him that if he made the change he would rediscover in the other object the pleasure that he has renounced. If he comes to be treated at all, it is mostly through the pressure of external motives, such as the social disadvantages and dangers attaching to his choice of object, and such components of the instinct of self-preservation prove themselves too weak in the struggle against the sexual impulsions. One then soon discovers his secret plan, namely, to obtain from the striking failure of his attempt a feeling of satisfaction that he has done everything possible against his abnormality, to which he can now resign himself with an easy conscience. The case is somewhat different when consideration for beloved parents and relatives has been the motive for his attempt to be cured. Here there really are libidinal impulsions present which may put forth energies opposed to the homosexual choice of object; but their strength is rarely sufficient. It is only where the homosexual fixation has not yet become strong enough, or where there are considerable rudiments and vestiges of a heterosexual choice of object, i.e. in a still oscillating or in a definitely bisexual organization, that one may make a more favourable prognosis for psycho-analytic therapy. . . .

Readers unversed in psycho-analysis will long have been awaiting an answer to two other questions. Did this homosexual girl show physical characteristics plainly belonging to the opposite sex, and did the case prove to be one of congenital or acquired (later-developed) homosexuality?

I am aware of the importance attaching to the first of these questions. But one should not exaggerate it and allow it to overshadow the fact that sporadic secondary characteristics of the opposite sex are very often present in normal individuals, and that well-marked physical characteristics of the opposite sex may be found in persons whose choice of object has undergone no change in the direction of inversion; in other words, that in both sexes *the degree of physical hermaphroditism is to a great extent independent of psychical hermaphroditism.* In modification of these statements it must be added that this independence is more evident in men than women, where bodily and mental traits belonging to the opposite sex are apt to coincide. Still I am not in a position to give a satisfactory answer to the first of our questions about my patient. The psycho-analyst customarily forgoes a thorough physical examination of his patients in certain cases. Certainly there was no obvious deviation from the feminine physical type, nor any menstrual disturbance. The beautiful and well-made girl had, it is true, her father's tall figure, and her facial features were sharp rather than soft and girlish, traits which might be regarded as indicating a physical masculinity. Some of her intellectual attributes also could be connected with masculinity: for instance, her acuteness of comprehension and her lucid objectivity, in so far as she was not dominated by her passion. But these distinctions are conventional rather than scientific. What is certainly of greater importance is that in her behaviour towards her love-object she had throughout assumed the masculine part: that is to say, she displayed the humility and the sublime overvaluation of the sexual object so characteristic of the male lover, the renunciation of all narcissistic satisfaction, and the preference for being the lover rather than the beloved. She had thus not only chosen a feminine love-object, but had also developed a masculine attitude towards that object.

Freud's analysis of the case recalls his strong belief in the influence of the mother-father-child triangle. As with the previous case, we see a basic framework (the Oedipal) but within which *various* scenarios may play out. Why do you think the patient's mother has been less disturbed by her daughter's behavior than the patient's father?

At the age of thirteen to fourteen she displayed a tender and, according to general opinion, exaggeratedly strong affection for a small boy, not quite three years old, whom she used to see regularly in a children's playground. She took to the child so warmly that in consequence a lasting friendship grew up between herself and his parents. One may infer from this episode that at that time she was possessed of a strong desire to be a mother herself and to have a child. However, after a short time she grew indifferent to the boy, and began to take an interest in mature, but still youthful, women. The manifestations of this interest soon brought upon her a severe chastisement at the hands of her father.

It was established beyond all doubt that this change occurred simultaneously with a certain event in the family, and one may therefore look to this for some explanation of the change. Before it happened, her libido was concentrated on a maternal attitude, while afterwards she became a homosexual attracted to mature women, and remained so ever since. The event which is so significant for our understanding of the case was a new pregnancy of her mother's, and the birth of a third brother when she was about sixteen.

The position of affairs which I shall now proceed to lay bare is not a product of my inventive powers; it is based on such trustworthy analytic evidence that I can claim objective validity for it. It was in particular a series of dreams, inter-related and easy to interpret, that decided me in favour of its reality.

The analysis revealed beyond all shadow of doubt that the lady-love was a substitute for—her mother. It is true that the lady herself was not a mother, but then she was not the girl's first love. The first objects of her affection after the birth of her youngest brother were really mothers, women between thirty and thirty-five whom she had met with their children during summer holidays or in the family circle of acquaintances in town. Motherhood as a *sine qua non*[1] in her love-object was later on given up, because that precondition was difficult to combine in real life with another one, which grew more and more important. The specially intense bond with her latest love had still another basis which the girl discovered quite easily one day. Her lady's slender figure, severe beauty, and downright manner reminded her of the brother who was a little older than herself. Her latest choice corresponded, therefore, not only to her feminine but also to her masculine ideal; it combined satisfaction of the homosexual tendency with that of the heterosexual one. It is well known that analysis of male homosexuals has in numerous cases revealed the same combination, which should warn us not to form too simple a conception of the nature and genesis of inversion, and to keep in mind the universal bisexuality of human beings.

But how are we to understand the fact that it was precisely the birth of a child who came late in the family (at a time when the girl herself was already mature and had strong wishes of her own) that moved her to bestow her passionate tenderness upon the woman who gave birth to this child, i.e. her own mother, and to express that feeling towards a substitute for her mother? From all that we know we should have expected just the opposite. In such circumstances mothers with daughters of nearly a marriageable age usually feel embarrassed in regard to them, while the daughters are apt to feel for their mothers a mixture of compassion, contempt and envy which does nothing to increase their tenderness for them. The girl we are considering had in any case altogether little cause to feel affection for her mother. The latter, still youthful herself, saw in her rapidly developing daughter an inconvenient competitor; she favoured the sons at her expense, limited her independence as much as possible, and kept an especially strict watch against any close relation between the girl and her father. A yearning from the beginning for a kinder mother would, therefore, have been quite intelligible, but why it should have flared up just then, and in the form of a consuming passion, is hard to understand.

The explanation is as follows. It was just when the girl was experiencing the revival of her infantile Oedipus complex at puberty that she suffered her great disappointment. She became keenly conscious of the wish to have a child, and a male one; that what she desired was her *father's* child and an image of *him*, her consciousness was not allowed to know. And what happened next? It was not *she* who bore the child, but her unconsciously hated rival, her mother. Furiously resentful and embittered, she turned away from her father and from men altogether. After this first great reverse she forswore her womanhood and sought another goal for her libido.

In doing so she behaved just as many men do who after a first distressing experience turn their backs for ever upon the faithless female sex and become woman-haters. It is related of one of the most attractive and unfortunate princely figures of our time that he became a homosexual because the lady he was engaged to marry betrayed him with another man. I do not know whether this is true historically, but an element of psychological truth lies behind the rumour. In all of us, throughout life, the libido normally oscillates between male and female objects; the bachelor gives up his men friends when he marries, and returns to club-life when married life has lost its savour. Naturally, when the swing-over is fundamental and final, we suspect the presence of some special factor which definitely favours one side or the other, and which perhaps has only waited for the appropriate moment in order to turn the choice of object in its direction.

After her disappointment, therefore, this girl had entirely repudiated her wish for a child, her love of men, and the feminine role in general. It is evident that at this point a number of very different things might have happened. What actually happened was the most extreme case. She changed into a man and took her mother in place of her father as the object of her love.[2] Her relation to her mother had certainly been ambivalent from the beginning, and it proved easy to revive her earlier love for her mother and with its help to bring about an overcompensation for her current hostility towards her. Since there was little to be done with the real mother, there arose from this transformation of feeling the search for a substitute mother to whom she could become passionately attached.[3]

There was, in addition, a practical motive for this change, derived from her real relations with her mother, which served as a [secondary] gain from her illness. The mother herself still attached great value to the attentions and the admiration of men. If, then, the girl became homosexual and left men to her mother (in other words, "retired in favour of" her mother), she would remove something which had hitherto been partly responsible for her mother's dislike.[4]

This libidinal position of the girl's, thus arrived at, was greatly reinforced as soon as she perceived how much it displeased her father. After she had been punished for her over-affectionate attitude to a woman she realized how she could wound her father and take revenge on him. Henceforth she remained homosexual out of defiance against her father. Nor did she scruple to lie to him and to deceive him in every way. Towards her mother, indeed, she was only so far deceitful as was necessary to prevent her father from knowing things. I had the impression that her behaviour followed the principle of the talion:[5] "Since you have betrayed me, you must put up with my betraying you." Nor can I come to any other conclusion about the striking lack of caution displayed by this otherwise exceedingly shrewd girl. She *wanted* her father to know occasionally of her relations with the lady, otherwise she would be deprived of the satisfaction of her keenest desire—namely, revenge. So she saw to this by showing herself openly in the company of her adored one, by walking with her in the streets near her father's place of business, and the like. This maladroitness, moreover, was by no means unintentional. It was remarkable, too, that both parents behaved as if they understood their daughter's secret psychology. The mother was tolerant, as though she appreciated her daughter's "retirement" as a favour to her; the father was furious, as though he realized the deliberate revenge directed against himself.

The girl's inversion, however, received its final reinforcement when she found in her "lady" an object which promised to satisfy not only her homosexual trends, but also that part of her heterosexual libido which was still attached to her brother.

> The following passages detail the concepts of resistance, transference, ambivalence, and denial. Freud makes an interesting distinction between dreams and the unconscious, and he furthers his (often ignored) implication that each case is unique.

In the girl's account of her conscious motives the father did not figure at all; there was not even any mention of fear of his anger. In the motives laid bare by the analysis, on the other hand, he played the principal part. Her relation to her father had the same decisive importance for the course and outcome of the analytic treatment, or rather, analytic exploration. Behind her pretended consideration for her parents, for whose sake she had been willing to make the attempt to be transformed, lay concealed her attitude of defiance and revenge against her father which held her fast to her homosexuality. Secure under this cover, the resistance set a considerable region free to analytic investigation. The analysis went forward almost without any signs of resistance, the patient participating actively with her intellect, though absolutely tranquil emotionally. Once when I expounded to her a specially important part of the theory, one touching her nearly, she replied in an inimitable tone, "How very interesting," as though she were a *grande dame* being taken over a museum and glancing through her lorgnon at objects to which she was completely indifferent. The impression one had of her analysis was not unlike that of a hypnotic treatment, where the resistance has in the same way withdrawn to a certain boundary line, beyond which it proves to be unconquerable. The resistance very often pursues similar tactics—Russian tactics, as they might be called—in cases of obsessional neurosis. For a time, consequently, these cases yield the clearest results and permit a deep insight into the causation of the symptoms. But presently one begins to wonder how it is that such marked progress in analytic understanding can be unaccompanied by even the slightest change in the patient's compulsions and inhibitions, until at last one perceives that everything that has been accomplished is subject to a mental reservation of doubt, and that behind this protective barrier the neurosis can feel secure. "It would be all very fine," thinks the patient, often quite consciously, "if I were obliged to believe what the man says, but there is no question of that, and so long as this is so I need change nothing." Then, when one comes to close quarters with the motives for this doubt, the fight with the resistances breaks out in earnest.

In the case of our patient, it was not doubt but the affective factor of revenge against her father that made her cool reserve possible, that divided the analysis into two distinct phases, and rendered the results of the first phase so complete and perspicuous. It seemed, further, as though nothing resembling a transference to the physician had been effected. That, however, is of course absurd, or, at least, is a loose way of expressing things. For some kind of relation to the analyst must come into being, and this relation is almost always transferred from an infantile one. In reality she transferred to me the sweeping repudiation of men which had dominated her ever since the disappointment she had suffered from her father. Bitterness against men is as a rule easy to gratify upon the physician; it need not evoke any violent emotional manifestations; it simply expresses itself by rendering futile all his endeavours and by clinging to the illness. I know from experience how difficult it is to make a patient understand just precisely this mute kind of symptomatic behaviour and to make him aware of this latent, and often exceedingly strong, hostility without endangering the treatment. As soon, therefore, as I recognized the girl's attitude to her father, I broke off the treatment and advised her parents that if they set store by the therapeutic procedure it should be continued by a woman doctor. The girl had in the meanwhile promised her father that at any rate she would give up seeing the "lady," and I do not know whether my advice, the reasons for which are obvious, will be followed.

There was a single piece of material in the course of this analysis which I could regard as a positive transference, as a greatly weakened revival of the girl's original passionate love for her father. Even this manifestation was not quite free from other motives, but I mention it because it brings up, in another direction, an interesting problem of analytic technique. At a certain period, not long after the treatment had begun, the girl brought a series of dreams which, distorted according to rule and couched in the usual dream-language, could nevertheless be easily translated with certainty. Their content, when interpreted, was, however, remarkable. They anticipated the cure of the inversion through the treatment, expressed her joy over the prospects in life that would then be opened before her, confessed her longing for a man's love and for children, and so might have been welcomed as a gratifying preparation for the desired change. The contradiction between them and the girl's utterances in waking life at the time was very great. She did not conceal from me that she meant to marry, but only in order to escape from her father's tyranny and to follow her true inclinations undisturbed. As for the husband, she remarked rather contemptuously, she would easily deal with him, and besides, one could have sexual relations with a man and a woman at one and the same time, as the example of the adored lady showed. Warned through some slight impression or other, I told her one day that I did not believe these dreams, that I regarded them as false or hypocritical, and that she intended to deceive me just as she habitually deceived her father. I was right; after I had made this clear, this kind of dream ceased. But I still believe that, beside the intention to mislead me, the dreams partly expressed the wish to win my favour; they were also an attempt to gain my interest and my good opinion—perhaps in order to disappoint me all the more thoroughly later on.

I can imagine that to point out the existence of lying dreams of this kind, "obliging" dreams, will arouse a positive storm of helpless indignation in some readers who call themselves analysts. "What!" they will exclaim, "the unconscious, the real centre of our mental life, the part of us that is so much nearer the divine than our poor consciousness—it too can lie! Then how can we still build on the interpretations of analysis and the accuracy of our findings?" To which one must reply that the recognition of these lying dreams does not constitute any shattering novelty. I know, indeed, that the craving of mankind for mysticism is ineradicable, and that it makes ceaseless efforts to win back for mysticism the territory it has been deprived of by *The Interpretation of Dreams*, but surely in the case under consideration everything is simple enough. A dream is not the "unconscious"; it is the form into which a thought left over from preconscious, or even from conscious, waking life, can, thanks to the favouring state of sleep, be recast. In the state of sleep this thought has been reinforced by unconscious wishful impulses and has thus experienced distortion through the dream-work, which is determined by the mechanisms prevailing in the unconscious. With our dreamer, the intention to mislead me, just as she did her father, certainly emanated from the preconscious, and may indeed have been conscious; it could come to expression by entering into connection with the unconscious wishful impulse to please her father (or father-substitute), and in this way it created a lying dream. The two intentions, to betray and to please her father, originated in the same complex; the former resulted from the repression of the latter, and the later one was brought back by the dream-work to the earlier one. There can therefore be no question of any devaluation of the unconscious, nor of a shattering of our confidence in the results of analysis.

I cannot neglect this opportunity of expressing for once my astonishment that human beings can go through such great and important moments of their erotic life without noticing them much, sometimes even, indeed, without having the faintest suspicion of their existence, or else, having become aware of those moments, deceive themselves so thoroughly in their judgment of them. This happens not only under neurotic conditions, where we are familiar with the phenomenon, but seems also to be common enough in ordinary life. In the present case, for example, a girl develops a sentimental adoration for women, which her parents at first find merely vexatious and hardly take seriously; she herself knows quite well that she is very much occupied with these relationships, but still she experiences few of the sensations of intense love until a particular frustration is followed by a quite excessive reaction, which shows everyone concerned that they have to do with a consuming passion of elemental strength. Nor had the girl ever perceived anything of the state of affairs which was a necessary preliminary to the outbreak of this mental storm. In other cases, too, we come across girls or women in a state of severe depression, who on being asked for a possible cause of their condition tell us that they have, it is true, had a slight feeling for a certain person, but that it was nothing deep and that they soon got over it when they had to give it up. And yet it was this renunciation, apparently so easily borne, that became the cause of serious mental disturbance. Again, we come across men who have passed through casual love-affairs and realize only from the subsequent effects that they had been passionately in love with the person whom they had apparently regarded lightly. One is also amazed at the unexpected results that may follow an artificial abortion, the killing of an unborn child, which had been decided upon without remorse and without hesitation. It must be admitted that poets are right in liking to portray people who are in love without knowing it, or uncertain whether they do love, or who think that they hate when in reality they love. It would seem that the information received by our consciousness about our erotic life is especially liable to be incomplete, full of gaps, or falsified. Needless to say, in this discussion I have not omitted to allow for the part played by subsequent forgetting. . . .

We do not, therefore, mean to maintain that every girl who experiences a disappointment such as this of the longing for love that springs from the Oedipus attitude at puberty will necessarily on that account fall a victim to homosexuality. On the contrary, other kinds of reaction to this trauma are undoubtedly commoner. If so, however, there must have been present in this girl special factors that turned the scale, factors outside the trauma, probably of an internal nature. Nor is there any difficulty in pointing them out.

Female Sexuality

Although he treated a large number of female patients, Freud's work concerning women is thin. The case we just read offers some account of the female Oedipal phase and its ramifications. *Female Sexuality* gives a more thorough and detailed account of the Oedipal in women. Freud focuses on the pre-Oedipal period in women more than he does in men. He asserts that the biology of a woman manifests in a number of possible social/sexual orientations. As the previous case attests, we know that the cause of one result rather than another has much to do with the unique situation of each individual.

In that phase of children's libidinal development which is characterized by the normal Oedipus complex we find that they are tenderly attached to the parent of the opposite sex, while their relation to the other parent is predominantly hostile. In the case of boys the explanation is simple. A boy's mother was his first love-object; she remains so, and, as his feeling for her becomes more passionate and he understands more of the relation between father and mother, the former inevitably appears as a rival. With little girls it is otherwise. For them, too, the mother was the first love-object; how then does a little girl find her way to her father? How, when and why does she detach herself from her mother? We have long realized that in women the development of sexuality is complicated by the task of renouncing that genital zone which was originally the principal one, namely, the clitoris, in favour of a new zone—the vagina. But there is a second change which appears to us no less characteristic and important for feminine development: the original mother-object has to be exchanged for the father. We cannot as yet see clearly how these two tasks are linked up.

We know that women with a strong father-attachment are numerous and not by any means neurotic. In studying this type I have made some observations which I propose to communicate here and which have led me to a certain view of female sexuality. I have been struck, above all, by two facts. First, analysis has shown that where

The excerpts in this section are taken from Sigmund Freud's *Female Sexuality*, in *Collected Papers*, Vol. 5, edited by James Strachey (London: Hogarth Press and Institute of Psycho-Analysis, 1950), pp. 252–261, by arrangement with Paterson Marsh Ltd., London.

the attachment to the father was peculiarly strong it had been preceded by a phase of equally strong and passionate attachment exclusively to the mother. Except for the change in the object, the love-life had acquired hardly a single new feature in the second phase. The primary mother-relation had developed in a very rich and many-sided way.

Secondly, I learnt that the duration of this attachment to the mother had been greatly underestimated. In a number of cases it persisted well into the fourth and, in one, into the fifth year, so that it comprised by far the longer period of the early sexual efflorescence. Indeed, one had to give due weight to the possibility that many a woman may remain arrested at the original mother-attachment and never properly achieve the change-over to men.

These facts show that the pre-Oedipus phase in women is more important than we have hitherto supposed.

Since there is time during this phase for all the fixations and repressions which we regard as the source of the neurosis, it seems that we shall have to retract the universality of the dictum that the Oedipus complex is the nucleus of neurosis. But if anyone feels reluctant to adopt this correction, he need not do so. For, on the one hand, we can extend the content of the Oedipus complex to include all the child's relations to both parents or, on the other, we can give due recognition to our new findings by saying that women reach the normal, positive Oedipus situation only after surmounting a first phase dominated by the negative complex. Actually, during this phase, to a little girl, her father is not very different from a troublesome rival even though her hostility towards him never reaches such a pitch as does the boy's. We have, after all, long given up any expectation of a neat parallelism between the male and female sexual development.

Our insight into this early, pre-Oedipus phase in the little girl's development comes to us as a surprise, comparable in another field with the effect of the discovery of the Minoan-Mycenaean civilization behind that of Greece. . . .

I have begun by stating the two facts which have struck me as new; first, that the great dependence on the father in women merely takes over the heritage of an equally great attachment to the mother and, secondly, that this earlier phase lasts longer than we should have anticipated. I must now go back a little in order to insert these new conclusions in their proper place in the picture of female sexual development with which we are already familiar. A certain amount of repetition is here inevitable. It will help our exposition if, as we go along, we compare the course of female development with that of the male.

First of all, there can be no doubt that the bisexual disposition which we maintain to be characteristic of human beings manifests itself much more plainly in the female than in the male. The latter has only one principal sexual zone—only one sexual organ—whereas the former has two: the vagina, the true female organ, and the clitoris, which is analogous to the male organ. We believe that we may justly assume that for many years the vagina is virtually non-existent and possibly remains without sensation until puberty. It is true, however, that recently an increasing number of observers have been inclined to think that vaginal stirrings are present even in those early years. In any case female genitality must, in childhood, centre principally in the clitoris. The sexual life of the woman is regularly split up into two phases, the first of which is of a masculine character, whilst the second is specifically feminine. Thus in female development there is a process of transition from the one phase to the other, to which there is nothing analogous in males. A further complication arises from the fact that the clitoris, with its masculine character, continues to function in later female sexual life in a very variable manner, which we certainly do not as yet fully understand. Of course, we do not know what are the biological roots of these specific characteristics of the woman, and we are still less able to assign to them any teleological purpose.

Parallel with this first great difference there is another, which concerns the love-object. The first love-object of the male is the mother, because it is she who feeds and tends him, and she remains his principal love-object until she is replaced by another which resembles her or is derived from her. With the female too the mother must be the first object, for the primary conditions of object-choice are the same for all children. But at the end of the girl's development it is the man—the father—who must come to be the new love object; *i.e.* as she changes in sex, so must the sex of her love-object change. What we now have to discover is how this transformation takes place, how radical or how incomplete it is, and all the different things that may happen in this process of development.

We have already observed that there is yet another difference between the sexes in their relation to the Oedipus complex. We have the impression that what we have said about that complex applies in all strictness only to male children, and that we are right in rejecting the term "Electra complex" which seeks to insist that the situation of the two sexes is analogous. It is only in male children that there occurs the fateful simultaneous conjunction of love for the one parent and hatred of the other as rival. It is thereupon the discovery of the possibility of castration, as evidenced by the sight of the female genital, which necessitates the transformation of the boy's Oedipus complex, leads to the creation of the super-ego and thus initiates all the processes that culminate in enrolling the individual in civilized society. After the paternal function has been internalized so as to form the super-ego, the next task is to detach the latter from those persons of whom it was originally the psychical representative. In this remarkable course of development the agent employed to restrain infantile sexuality is precisely that narcissistic genital interest which centres in the preservation of the penis.

One residue of the castration complex in the man is a measure of disparagement in his attitude towards women, whom he regards as having been castrated. In extreme cases this inhibits his object-choice, and, if reinforced by organic factors, it may result in exclusive homosexuality. Very different is the effect of the castration complex on the girl. She acknowledges the fact of her castration, the consequent superiority of the male and her own inferiority, but she also rebels against these unpleasant facts. So divided in her mind, she may follow one of three lines of development. The first leads to her turning her back on sexuality altogether. The budding woman, frightened by the comparison of herself with boys, becomes dissatisfied with her clitoris and gives up her phallic activity and therewith her sexuality in general and a considerable part of her masculine proclivities in other fields. If she pursues the second line, she clings in obstinate self-assertion to her threatened masculinity; the hope of getting a penis sometime is cherished to an incredibly late age and becomes the aim of her life, whilst the phantasy of really being a man, in spite of everything, often dominates long periods of her life. This "masculinity complex" may also result in a manifestly homosexual object-choice. Only if her development follows the third, very circuitous path does she arrive at the ultimate normal feminine attitude in which she takes her father as love-object, and thus arrives at the Oedipus complex in its feminine form. Thus, in women, that complex represents the final result of a lengthy process of development; castration does not destroy but rather creates it, and it escapes the strong hostile influences which, in men, tend to its destruction—in fact, only too often a woman never surmounts it at all. Hence too the cultural effects of the break-up of this complex are slighter and less important in women than in men. We should probably not err in saying that it is this difference in the interrelation of the Oedipus and the castration-complexes which gives its special stamp to the character of woman as a member of society.[1]

> The next passage explains why a young girl will replace her original love-object (mother) with her father, but her wishes will not be fulfilled. Freud implies, as the previous case attests, that a woman's relations to men are heavily influenced by her emotions toward her mother and the attempts to identify with her father.

We see then that the phase of exclusive attachment to the mother, which may be called the *pre-Oedipus* phase, is far more important in women than it can claim to be in men. Many phenomena of feminine sexual life which were difficult to understand before can be fully explained by reference to this phase. For example, we had noted long ago that many a woman who takes her father as the model for her choice of a husband, or assigns her father's place to him, yet in her married life repeats with her husband her bad relations with her mother. He should have succeeded to her relation with her father, but in reality he takes over her relation to her mother. This is easily explained as an obvious case of regression. The mother-relation was the original one, upon which the father-relation was built up; in married life the original basis emerges from repression. For her development to womanhood consisted mainly in transferring affective ties from the mother to the father-object.

With many women we have the impression that the period of their maturity is entirely taken up with conflicts with their husbands, just as they spent their youth in conflicts with their mothers. In the light of what I have now said we shall conclude that the hostile attitude to the mother is not a consequence of the rivalry implicit in the Oedipus complex, but rather originates in the preceding phase and has simply found in the Oedipus situation reinforcement and an opportunity for asserting itself. Direct analytic investigation confirms this view. Our interest must be directed to the mechanisms at work in the turning away from the mother-object, originally so vehemently and exclusively loved. We are prepared to find not one solitary factor but a whole number of these contributing to the same end.

Amongst these factors are some which are conditioned by the circumstances of infantile sexuality in general and so hold good equally for the love-relations of boys. First and foremost we must mention jealousy of other persons—brothers and sisters and rivals, amongst whom is also the father. Childish love knows no bounds, it demands exclusive possession, is satisfied with nothing less than all. But it has a second characteristic: it has no real aim; it is incapable of complete satisfaction and this is the principal reason why it is doomed to end in disappointment and to give place to a hostile attitude. Later on in life, the lack of ultimate gratification may conduce to a different result. This very factor may ensure the undisturbed continuance of the libidal cathexis, as is the case in love-relations inhibited in their aim. But in the stress of the processes of development it regularly happens that the libido abandons its unsatisfactory position in order to find a new one.

There is another, far more specific motive for the turning away from the mother, arising out of the effect of the castration-complex on the little creature without a penis. Some time or other the little girl makes the discovery of her organic inferiority, of course earlier and more easily if she has brothers or other boy companions. We have already noted the three paths which diverge from this point: *(a)* that which leads to the suspension of the whole sexual life, *(b)* that which leads to the defiant over-emphasis of her own masculinity, and *(c)* the first steps towards definitive femininity. It is not easy to say precisely when these processes occur or to lay down their typical course. Even the point of time when the discovery of castration is made varies and many other factors seem to be inconstant and to depend on chance. The condition of the girl's own phallic-activity plays a part, as also whether it is discovered or not, and how far it is hindered after the discovery.

The little girl generally finds out spontaneously her mode of phallic activity— masturbation of the clitoris—and in the first instance it is no doubt unaccompanied by phantasies. The way in which the tending of the child's body influences the awakening of this activity is reflected in the very common phantasy of seduction by her mother, her wet-nurse or nursemaid. Whether little girls practise masturbation more rarely and from the beginning less energetically than little boys is a point which we must leave undecided: quite possibly this is the case. Actual seduction is likewise common enough, either at the hands of other children or of nurses who want to soothe the child, send her to sleep or make her dependent on them. Where seduction intervenes, it invariably disturbs the natural course of development and often has profound and lasting consequences.

The prohibition of masturbation may, as we have seen, act as an incentive for giving the habit up, but it may also operate as a motive for rebellion against the person who forbids, i.e. the mother, or the mother-substitute who later regularly merges into the mother. The defiant persistence in masturbation would appear to open the way to masculinity. Even when the child does not succeed in mastering her habit, the effect of the apparently unavailing prohibition is seen in her later efforts to free herself at all costs from a gratification which has been made distasteful to her. When the girl reaches maturity her object-choice may still be influenced by this firmly maintained purpose. Resentment at being prevented from free sexual activity has much to do with her detachment from her mother. The same motive recurs after puberty when the mother takes up the duty of protecting her daughter's chastity. Of course, we must remember here that the mother opposes masturbation in the boy in the same way, thus providing him also with a powerful motive for rebellion.

When a little girl has sight of a male genital organ and so discovers her own deficiency, she does not accept the unwelcome knowledge without hesitation and reluctance. As we have seen, she clings obstinately to the expectation of acquiring a similar organ sometime, and the desire for it survives long after the hope is extinguished. Invariably the child regards castration in the first instance as a misfortune peculiar to herself; only later does she realize that it extends to certain other children and at length to certain adults. When the universality of this negative character of her sex dawns upon her, womanhood, and with it also her mother, suffers a heavy loss of credit in her eyes.

Very possibly this account of the little girl's reaction to her impression of castration and the prohibition of masturbation will strike the reader as confused and contradictory. That is not altogether the writer's fault. A description which fits every case is in fact almost impossible. In different individuals we find the most various reactions; even in the same individual contrary attitudes exist side by side. With the first intervention of the prohibition there begins a conflict which from that moment will accompany the development of the sexual function. It is particularly difficult to get a clear insight into what takes place because it is so hard to distinguish the mental processes of this first phase from the later ones by which they become overlaid and distorted in memory. For example, the fact of castration is sometimes construed later as a punishment for masturbation, and its infliction is ascribed to the father; of course, neither of these ideas can be the original one. With boys also it is regularly the father from whom castration is dreaded, although in their case, as in the little girl's, it is mostly the mother who utters the threat.

The Dissolution of the Oedipus Complex

After reading and thinking about the following excerpt, try to answer this question: Does Freud believe, as he does for men, that the Oedipal events determine significant attitudes, roles, and traits for women in later stages of life?

The fear of castration being thus excluded in the little girl, a powerful motive also drops out for the setting-up of a super-ego and for the breaking-off of the infantile genital organization. In her, far more than in the boy, these changes seem to be the result of upbringing and of intimidation from outside which threatens her with a loss of love. The girl's Oedipus complex is much simpler than that of the small bearer of the penis; in my experience, it seldom goes beyond the taking of her mother's place and the adopting of a feminine attitude towards her father. Renunciation of the penis is not tolerated by the girl without some attempt at compensation. She slips—along the line of a symbolic equation, one might say—from the penis to the baby. Her Oedipus complex culminates in a desire, which is long retained, to receive a baby from her father as a gift—to bear him a child. One has an impression that the Oedipus complex is then gradually given up because this wish is never fulfilled. The two wishes—to possess a penis and a child—remain strongly cathected in the unconscious and help to prepare the female creature for her later sexual role. The comparatively lesser strength of the sadistic contribution to the sexual instinct, which we may no doubt connect with the stunted growth of her penis, makes it easier in her case for the direct sexual trends to be transformed in aim-inhibited trends of an affectionate kind. It must be admitted, however, that in general our insight into these developmental processes in girls is unsatisfactory, incomplete, and vague.

This excerpt is taken from Sigmund Freud's *The Dissolution of the Oedipus Complex*, edited and translated by James Strachey, in *Standard Edition of the Complete Psychological Works of Sigmund Freud*, Vol. 19 (London: Hogarth Press and Institute of Psycho-Analysis, 1961), pp. 178–179, by arrangement with Paterson Marsh Ltd., London.

Part Two

Psychoanalytic Interpretations of Culture

Our exploration of Freud has focused almost entirely on his theories in relation to the individual. The four works excerpted here attempt to apply psychoanalytic concepts to social and cultural life. The following thoughts may serve as a starting point:

1. *Psychological tendencies, while individually unique, reflect universal desires.*

2. *When individuals associate or identify with something larger, they do so according to both their personal and human psychology.*

Totem and Taboo

In *Totem and Taboo,* Freud speculates about a single event which gave primitive humans the impetus to create civilization. He begins by studying past and present totemic clans, and is struck by the breadth of their incest taboos.

THE HORROR OF INCEST

Prehistoric man, in the various stages of his development, is known to us through the inanimate monuments and implements which he has left behind, through the information about his art, his religion and his attitude towards life which has come to us either directly or by way of tradition handed down in legends, myths and fairy tales, and through the relics of his mode of thought which survive in our own manners and customs. But apart from this, in a certain sense he is still our contemporary. There are men still living who, as we believe, stand very near to primitive man, far nearer than we do, and whom we therefore regard as his direct heirs and representatives. Such is our view of those whom we describe as savages or half-savages; and their mental life must have a peculiar interest for us if we are right in seeing in it a well-preserved picture of an early stage of our own development.

If that supposition is correct, a comparison between the psychology of primitive peoples, as it is taught by social anthropology, and the psychology of neurotics, as it has been revealed by psycho-analysis, will be bound to show numerous points of agreement and will throw new light upon familiar facts in both sciences.

For external as well as for internal reasons, I shall select as the basis for this comparison the tribes which have been described by anthropologists as the most backward and miserable of savages, the aborigines of Australia, the youngest continent, in whose fauna, too, we can still observe much that is archaic and that has perished elsewhere.

The Australian aborigines are regarded as a distinct race, showing neither physical nor linguistic relationship with their nearest neighbours, the Melanesian, Polynesian and Malayan peoples. They do not build houses or permanent shelters; they do not cultivate the soil; they keep no domesticated animals except the dog; they are not even acquainted with the art of making pottery. They live entirely upon the flesh of all kinds of animals which they hunt, and upon roots which they dig. Kings or chiefs are unknown among them; communal affairs are decided by a council of elders. It is highly doubtful whether any religion, in the shape of a worship of higher beings, can be attributed to them. The tribes in the interior of the continent, who have to struggle against the hardest conditions of existence as a result of the scarcity of water, appear to be more primitive in all respects than those living near the coast.

We should certainly not expect that the sexual life of these poor, naked cannibals would be moral in our sense or that their sexual instincts would be subjected to any great degree of restriction. Yet we find that they set before themselves with the most scrupulous care and the most painful severity the aim of avoiding incestuous sexual relations. Indeed, their whole social organization seems to serve that purpose or to have been brought into relation with its attainment.

Among the Australians the place of all the religious and social institutions which they lack is taken by the system of "totemism." Australian tribes fall into smaller divisions, or clans, each of which is named after its totem. What is a totem? It is as a rule an animal (whether edible and harmless or dangerous and feared) and more rarely a plant or a natural phenomenon (such as rain or water), which stands in a peculiar relation to the whole clan. In the first place, the totem is the common ancestor of the clan; at the same time it is their guardian spirit and helper, which sends them oracles and, if dangerous to others, recognizes and spares its own children. Conversely, the clansmen are under a sacred obligation (subject to automatic sanctions) not to kill or destroy their totem and to avoid eating its flesh (or deriving benefit from it in other ways). The totemic character is inherent, not in some individual animal or entity, but in all the individuals of a given class. From time to time festivals are celebrated at which the clansmen represent or imitate the motions and attributes of their totem in ceremonial dances.

The totem may be inherited either through the female or through the male line. It is possible that originally the former method of descent prevailed everywhere and was only subsequently replaced by the latter. An Australian's relation to his totem is the basis of all his social obligations: it overrides on the one hand his tribal membership and on the other hand his blood relationships.[1]

The totem is not attached to one particular place. The clansmen are distributed in different localities and live peacefully side by side with members of other totem clans.[2]

And now we come at last to the characteristic of the totemic system which has attracted the interest of psycho-analysts. In almost every place where we find totems we also find a law against persons of the same totem having sexual relations with one another and consequently against their marrying. This, then, is "exogamy," an institution related to totemism.

Strictly enforced as it is, this prohibition is a remarkable one. There is nothing in the concept or attributes of the totem which I have so far mentioned to lead us to anticipate it; so that it is hard to understand how it has become involved in the totemic system. We cannot, therefore, feel surprised that some investigators actually suppose that exogamy had originally—in the earliest times and in its true meaning—nothing to do with totemism, but became attached to it (without there being any underlying connection) at some time when marriage restrictions became necessary. However this may be, the bond between totemism and exogamy exists and is clearly a very firm one.

Some further considerations will make the significance of this prohibition clearer:

(a) The violation of the prohibition is not left to what might be called the "automatic" punishment of the guilty parties, as in the case of other totem prohibitions, such as that against killing the totem animal. It is avenged in the most energetic fashion by the whole clan, as though it were a question of averting some danger that threatened the whole community or some guilt that was pressing upon it. A few sentences from Frazer (1910, 1, 54) will show how severely such misdeeds are treated by savages who are otherwise far from being moral by our standards:

"In Australia the regular penalty for sexual intercourse with a person of a forbidden clan is death. It matters not whether the woman be of the same local group or has been captured in war from another tribe; a man of the wrong clan who uses her as his wife is hunted down and killed by his clansmen, and so is the woman; though in some cases, if they succeed in eluding capture for a certain time, the offence may be condoned. In the Ta-ta-thi tribe, New South Wales, in the rare cases which occur, the man is killed but the woman is only beaten or speared, or both, till she is nearly dead; the reason given for not actually killing her being that she was probably coerced. Even in casual amours the clan prohibitions are strictly observed; any violations of these prohibitions 'are regarded with the utmost abhorrence and are punished by death.'" [Quoted from Cameron (1885, 351.)]

(b) Since the same severe punishment is inflicted in the case of passing love-affairs which have not resulted in any children, it seems unlikely that the reasons for the prohibition are of a practical nature.

(c) Since totems are hereditary and not changed by marriage, it is easy to follow the consequences of the prohibition. Where, for instance, descent is through the female line, if a man of the Kangaroo totem marries a woman of the Emu totem, all the children, both boys and girls, belong to the Emu clan. The totem regulation will therefore make it impossible for a son of this marriage to have incestuous intercourse with his mother or sisters, who are Emus like himself.[3]

(d) But a little more reflection will show that exogamy linked with the totem effects more (and therefore *aims* at more) than the prevention of incest with a man's mother and sisters. It makes sexual intercourse impossible for a man with all the women of his own clan (that is to say with a number of women who are not his blood-relatives) by treating them all as though they *were* his blood relatives. It is difficult at first sight to see the psychological justification for this very extensive restriction, which goes far beyond anything comparable among civilized peoples. It may be gathered from this, however, that the part played by the totem as common ancestor is taken very seriously. All those who are descended from the same totem are blood-relations. They form a single family, and within that family even the most distant degree of kinship is regarded as an absolute hindrance to sexual intercourse.

We see, then, that these savages have an unusually great horror of incest, or are sensitive on the subject to an unusual degree, and that they combine this with a peculiarity which remains obscure to us—of replacing real blood-relationship by totem kinship. This latter contrast must not, however, be too much exaggerated, and we must remember that the totem prohibitions include that against real incest as a special case.

> In search of the origin of incest taboos, Freud draws on archaeologist Robertson Smith's description and theory of the events of the totem meal. It is difficult to not be perplexed by the apparently contradictory progression of the totem event. What does the eating of the slaughtered animal remind us of?

Let us call up the spectacle of a totem meal of the kind we have been discussing, amplified by a few probable features which we have not yet been able to consider. The clan is celebrating the ceremonial occasion by the cruel slaughter of its totem animal and is devouring it raw—blood, flesh and bones. The clansmen are there, dressed in the likeness of the totem and imitating it in sound and movement, as though they are seeking to stress their identity with it. Each man is conscious that he is performing an act forbidden to the individual and justifiable only through the participation of the whole clan; nor may anyone absent himself from the killing and the meal. When the deed is done, the slaughtered animal is lamented and bewailed. The mourning is obligatory, imposed by dread of a threatened retribution. As Robertson Smith (1894, 412) remarks of an analogous occasion, its chief purpose is to disclaim responsibility for the killing.

But the mourning is followed by demonstrations of festive rejoicing: every instinct is unfettered and there is license for every kind of gratification. Here we have easy access to an understanding of the nature of festivals in general. A festival is a permitted, or rather an obligatory, excess, a solemn breach of a prohibition. It is not that men commit the excesses because they are feeling happy as a result of some injunction they have received. It is rather that excess is of the essence of a festival; the festive feeling is produced by the liberty to do what is as a rule prohibited.

What are we to make, though, of the prelude to this festive joy—the mourning over the death of the animal? If the clansmen rejoice over the killing of the totem—a normally forbidden act—why do they mourn it as well?

As we have seen, the clansmen acquire sanctity by consuming the totem: they reinforce their identification with it and with one another. Their festive feelings and all that follows from them might well be explained by the fact that they have taken into themselves the sacred life of which the substance of the totem is the vehicle.

Freud, influenced by Darwin, theorizes that the totem meal recreates the unfolding of events in the "primal horde." We notice Freud's typological approach to human behavior; he believes that human beings, *individually,* want to dominate their environment. He further believes that humans naturally feel ambivalent toward those who actually do.

Psycho-analysis has revealed that the totem animal is in reality a substitute for the father; and this tallies with the contradictory fact that, though the killing of the animal is as a rule forbidden, yet its killing becomes a festive occasion—the fact that it is killed and yet mourned. The ambivalent emotional attitude, which to this day characterizes the father-complex in our children and which often persists into adult life, seems to extend to the totem animal in its capacity as substitute for the father.

If, now, we bring together the psychoanalytic translation of the totem with the fact of the totem meal and with Darwin's theories of the earliest state of human society, the possibility of a deeper understanding emerges—a glimpse of a hypothesis which may seem fantastic but which offers the advantage of establishing an unsuspected correlation between groups of phenomena that have hitherto been disconnected.[4]

There is, of course, no place for the beginnings of totemism in Darwin's primal horde. All that we find there is a violent and jealous father who keeps all the females for himself and drives away his sons as they grow up. This earliest state of society has never been an object of observation. The most primitive kind of organization that we actually come across—and one that is in force to this day in certain tribes—consists of bands of males; these bands are composed of members with equal rights and are subject to the restrictions of the totemic system, including inheritance through the mother. Can this form of organization have developed out of the other one? And if so along what lines?

> In the following passage, Freud links Darwin, Smith, and his own conjecture that the exiled sons of a primitive horde murdered their authoritative, possessive father and triggered the origins of morality. However, Freud emphasizes the ambivalent feelings that the sons have for their father after the murder. How and why have the sons made the totem an ideal father?
>
> One family therapy theory, *multigenerational transmission process,* argues that our psyches or behaviors are the product of events from the past generations of our families. Freud seems to take this concept farther back and links our lives with those of our common ancestors.

If we call the celebration of the totem meal to our help, we shall be able to find an answer. One day[5] the brothers who had been driven out came together, killed and devoured their father and so made an end of the patriarchal horde. United, they had the courage to do and succeeded in doing what would have been impossible for them individually. (Some cultural advance, perhaps, command over some new weapon, had given them a sense of superior strength.) Cannibal savages as they were, it goes without saying that they devoured their victim as well as killing him. The violent primal father had doubtless been the feared and envied model of each one of the company of brothers: and in the act of devouring him they accomplished their identification with him, and each one of them acquired a portion of his strength. The totem meal, which is perhaps mankind's earliest festival, would thus be a repetition and a commemoration of this memorable and criminal deed, which was the beginning of so many things—of social organization, or moral restrictions and of religion.[6]

In order that these latter consequences may seem plausible, leaving their premises on one side, we need only suppose that the tumultuous mob of brothers were filled with the same contradictory feelings which we can see at work in the ambivalent father-complexes of our children and of our neurotic patients. They hated their father, who presented such a formidable obstacle to their craving for power and their sexual desires; but they loved and admired him too. After they had got rid of him, had satisfied their hatred and had put into effect their wish to identify themselves with him, the affection which had all this time been pushed under was bound to make itself felt.[7] It did so in the form of remorse. A sense of guilt made its appearance, which in this instance coincided with the remorse felt by the whole group. The dead father became stronger than the living one had been—for events took the course we so often see them follow in human affairs to this day. What had up to then been prevented by his actual existence was thenceforward prohibited by the sons themselves, in accordance with the psychological procedure so familiar to us in psycho-analyses under the name of "deferred obedience." They revoked their deed by forbidding the killing of the totem, the substitute for their father; and they renounced its fruits by resigning their claim to the women who had now been set free. They thus created out of their filial sense of guilt the two fundamental taboos of totemism, which for that very reason inevitably corresponded to the two repressed wishes of the Oedipus complex. Whoever contravened those taboos became guilty of the only two crimes with which primitive society concerned itself.[8]

The two taboos of totemism with which human morality has its beginning are not on a par psychologically. The first of them, the law protecting the totem animal, is founded wholly on emotional motives: the father had actually been eliminated, and in no real sense could the deed be undone. But the second rule, the prohibition of incest, has a powerful practical basis as well. Sexual desires do not unite men but divide them. Though the brothers had banded together in order to overcome their father, they were all one another's rivals in regard to the women. Each of them would have wished, like his father, to have all the women to himself. The new organization would have collapsed in a struggle of all against all, for none of them was of such overmastering strength as to be able to take on his father's part with success. Thus the brothers had no alternative, if they were to live together, but—not, perhaps, until they had passed through many dangerous crises—to institute the law against incest, by which they all alike renounced the women whom they desired and who had been their chief motive for despatching their father. In this way they rescued the organization which had made them strong—and which may have been based on homosexual feelings and acts, originating perhaps during the period of their expulsion from the horde. Here, too, may perhaps have been the germ of the institution of matriarchy, described by Bachofen [1861], which was in turn replaced by the patriarchal organization of the family.

On the other hand, the claim of totemism to be regarded as a first attempt at a religion is based on the first of these two taboos—that upon taking the life of the totem animal. The animal struck the sons as a natural and obvious substitute for their father; but the treatment of it which they found imposed on themselves expressed more than the need to exhibit their remorse. They could attempt, in their relation to this surrogate father, to allay their burning sense of guilt, to bring about a kind of reconciliation with their father. The totemic system was, as it were, a covenant with their father, in which he promised them everything that a childish imagination may expect from a father—protection, care and indulgence—while on their side they undertook to respect his life, that is to say, not to repeat the deed which had brought destruction on their real father. Totemism, moreover, contained an attempt at self-justification: "If our father had treated us in the way the totem does, we should never have felt tempted to kill him." In this fashion totemism helped to smooth things over and to make it possible to forget the event to which it owed its origin.

Features were thus brought into existence which continued thenceforward to have a determining influence on the nature of religion. Totemic religion arose from the filial sense of guilt, in an attempt to allay that feeling and to appease the father by deferred obedience to him. All later religions are seen to be attempts at solving the same problem. They vary according to the stage of civilization at which they arise and according to the methods which they adopt; but all have the same end in view and are reactions to the same great event with which civilization began and which, since it occurred, has not allowed mankind a moment's rest.

There is another feature which was already present in totemism and which has been preserved unaltered in religion. The tension of ambivalence was evidently too great for any contrivance to be able to counteract it; or it is possible that psychological conditions in general are unfavourable to getting rid of these antithetical emotions. However that may be, we find that the ambivalence implicit in the father-complex persists in totemism and in religions generally. Totemic religion not only comprised expressions of remorse and attempts at atonement, it also served as a remembrance of the triumph over the father. Satisfaction over that triumph led to the institution of the memorial festival of the totem meal, in which the restrictions of deferred obedience no longer held. Thus it became a duty to repeat the crime of parricide again and again in the sacrifice of the totem animal, whenever, as a result of the changing conditions of life, the cherished fruit of the crime—appropriation of the paternal attributes— threatened to disappear. We shall not be surprised to find that the element of filial rebelliousness also emerges, in the *later* products of religion, often in the strangest disguises and transformations.

Hitherto we have followed the developments of the *affectionate* current of feeling towards the father, transformed into remorse, as we find them in religion and in moral ordinances (which are not sharply distinguished in totemism). But we must not overlook the fact that it was in the main with the impulses that led to parricide that the victory lay. For a long time afterwards, the social fraternal feelings, which were the basis of the whole transformation, continued to exercise a profound influence on the development of society. They found expression in the sanctification of the blood tie, in the emphasis upon the solidarity of all life within the same clan. In thus guaranteeing one another's lives, the brothers were declaring that no one of them must be treated by another as their father was treated by them all jointly. They were precluding the possibility of a repetition of their father's fate. To the religiously based prohibition against killing the totem was now added the socially based prohibition against fratricide. It was not until long afterwards that the prohibition ceased to be limited to members of the clan and assumed the simple form: "Thou shalt do no murder." The patriarchal horde was replaced in the first instance by the fraternal clan, whose existence was assured by the blood tie. Society was now based on complicity in the common crime; religion was based on the sense of guilt and the remorse attaching to it; while morality was based partly on the exigencies of this society and partly on the penance demanded by the sense of guilt.

> The myths mentioned in the next excerpt make us realize that Freud did not invent the Oedipus complex out of nothing. The parallels between the totem meal and the Christian Eucharist are compelling, as is the recurrence in many religious texts and myths of incidents of incest and violence occurring around important events. While Freud believed that the forms of human actions are subject to change, the parallels just pointed to suggest that humans are destined to repeat, individually and culturally, much the same story.

Thus psycho-analysis, in contradiction to the more recent views of the totemic system but in agreement with the earlier ones, requires us to assume that totemism and exogamy were intimately connected and had a simultaneous origin. . . .

A great number of powerful motives restrain me from any attempt at picturing the further development of religions from their origin in totemism to their condition today. I will only follow two threads whose course I can trace with especial clarity as they run through the pattern: the theme of the totemic sacrifice and the relation of son to father.

Robertson Smith has shown us that the ancient totem meal recurs in the original form of sacrifice. The meaning of the act is the same: sanctification through participation in a common meal. The sense of guilt, which can only be allayed by the solidarity of all the participants, also persists. What is new is the clan deity, in whose supposed presence the sacrifice is performed, who participates in the meal as though he were a clansman, and with whom those who consume the meal become identified. How does the god come to be in a situation to which he was originally a stranger?

The answer might be that in the meantime the concept of God had emerged—from some unknown source—and had taken control of the whole of religious life; and that, like everything else that was to survive, the totem meal had been obliged to find a point of contact with the new system. The psycho-analysis of individual human beings, however, teaches us with quite special insistence that the god of each of them is formed in the likeness of his father, that his personal relation to God depends on his relation to his father in the flesh and oscillates and changes along with that relation, and that at bottom God is nothing other than an exalted father. As in the case of totemism, psycho-analysis recommends us to have faith in the believers who call God their father, just as the totem was called the tribal ancestor. If psycho-analysis deserves any attention, then—without prejudice to any other sources or meanings of the concept of God, upon which psychoanalysis can throw no light—the paternal element in that concept must be a most important one. But in that case the father is represented twice over in the situation of primitive sacrifice: once as God and once as the totemic animal victim. And, even granting the restricted number of explanations open to psycho-analysis, one must ask whether this is possible and what sense it can have.

We know that there are a multiplicity of relations between the god and the sacred animal (the totem or the sacrificial victim). (1) Each god usually has an animal (and quite often several animals) sacred to him. (2) In the case of certain specially sacred sacrifices—"mystic" sacrifices—the victim was precisely the animal sacred to the god (Smith, 1894 [290]). (3) The god was often worshipped in the shape of an animal (or, to look at it in another way, animals were worshipped as gods) long after the age of totemism. (4) In myths the god often transforms himself into an animal, and frequently into the animal that is sacred to him.

It therefore seems plausible to suppose that the god himself was the totem animal, and that he developed out of it at a later stage of religious feeling. But we are relieved from the necessity for further discussion by the consideration that the totem is nothing other than a surrogate of the father. Thus, while the totem may be the *first* form of father-surrogate, the god will be a later one, in which the father has regained his human shape. A new creation such as this, derived from what constitutes the root of every form of religion—a longing for the father—might occur if in the process of time some fundamental change had taken place in man's relation to the father, and perhaps, too, in his relation to animals.

Signs of the occurrence of changes of this kind may easily be seen, even if we leave on one side the beginning of a mental estrangement from animals and the disrupting of totemism owing to domestication. . . . There was one factor in the state of affairs produced by the elimination of the father—which was bound in the course of time to cause an enormous increase in the longing felt for him. Each single one of the brothers who had banded together for the purpose of killing their father was inspired by a wish to become like him and had given expression to it by incorporating parts of their father's surrogate in the totem meal. But, in consequence of the pressure exercised upon each participant by the fraternal clan as a whole, that wish could not be fulfilled, For the future no one could or might ever again attain the father's supreme power, even though that was what all of them had striven for. Thus after a long lapse of time their bitterness against their father, which had driven them to their deed, grew less, and their longing for him increased; and it became possible for an ideal to emerge which embodied the unlimited power of the primal father against whom they had once fought as well as their readiness to submit to him. As a result of decisive cultural changes, the original democratic equality that had prevailed among all the individual clansmen became untenable; and there developed at the same time an inclination, based on veneration felt for particular human individuals, to revive the ancient paternal ideal by creating gods. The notion of a man becoming a god or of a god dying strikes us to-day as shockingly presumptuous; but even in classical antiquity there was nothing revolting in it.[9] The elevation of the father who had once been murdered into a god from whom the clan claimed descent was a far more serious attempt at atonement than had been the ancient covenant with the totem.

I cannot suggest at what point in this process of development a place is to be found for the great mother-goddesses, who may perhaps in general have preceded the father-gods. It seems certain, however, that the change in attitude to the father was not restricted to the sphere of religion but that it extended in a consistent manner to that other side of human life which had been affected by the father's removal—to social organization. With the introduction of father deities a fatherless society gradually changed into one organized on a patriarchal basis. The family was a restoration of the former primal horde and it gave back to fathers a large portion of their former rights. There were once more fathers, but the social achievements of the fraternal clan had not been abandoned; and the gulf between the new fathers of a family and the unrestricted primal father of the horde was wide enough to guarantee the continuance of the religious craving, the persistence of an unappeased longing for the father.

We see, then, that in the scene of sacrifice before the god of the clan the father *is* in fact represented twice over—as the god and as the totemic animal victim. But in our attempts at understanding this situation we must beware of interpretations which seek to translate it in a two-dimensional fashion as though it were an allegory, and which in so doing forget its historical stratification. The two-fold presence of the father corresponds to the two chronologically successive meanings of the scene. The ambivalent attitude towards the father has found a plastic expression in it, and so, too, has the victory of the son's affectionate emotions over his hostile ones. The scene of the father's vanquishment, of his greatest defeat, has become the stuff for the representation of the supreme triumph. The importance which is everywhere, without exception, ascribed to sacrifice lies in the fact that it offers satisfaction to the father for the outrage inflicted on him in the same act in which that deed is commemorated.

As time went on, the animal lost its sacred character and the sacrifice lost its connection with the totem feast; it became a simple offering to the deity, an act of renunciation in favour of the god. God Himself had become so far exalted above mankind that He could only be approached through an intermediary—the priest. At the same time divine kings made their appearance in the social structure and introduced the patriarchal system into the state. It must be confessed that the revenge taken by the deposed and restored father was a harsh one: the dominance of authority was at its climax. The subjugated sons made use of the new situation in order to unburden themselves still further of their sense of guilt. They were no longer in any way responsible for the sacrifice as it now was. It was God Himself who demanded it and regulated it.

This is the phase in which we find myths showing the god himself killing the animal which is sacred to him and which is in fact himself. Here we have the most extreme denial of the great crime which was the beginning of society and of the sense of guilt. But there is a second meaning to this last picture of sacrifice which is unmistakable. It expresses satisfaction at the earlier father-surrogate having been abandoned in favour of the superior concept of God. At this point the psychoanalytic interpretation of the scene coincides approximately with the allegorical, surface translation of it, which represents the god as overcoming the animal side of his own nature.[10]

Nevertheless it would be a mistake to suppose that the hostile impulses inherent in the father-complex were completely silenced during this period of revived paternal authority. On the contrary, the first phases of the dominance of the two new father-surrogates—gods and kings—show the most energetic signs of the ambivalence that remains a characteristic of religion.

In his great work, *The Golden Bough*, Frazer [1911, 2, chapter 18] puts forward the view that the earliest kings of the Latin tribes were foreigners who played the part of a god and were solemnly executed at a particular festival. The annual sacrifice (or, as a variant, self-sacrifice) of a god seems to have been an essential element in the Semitic religions. The ceremonials of human sacrifice, performed in the most different parts of the inhabited globe, leave very little doubt that the victims met their end as representatives of the deity; and these sacrificial rites can be traced into late times, with an inanimate effigy or puppet taking the place of the living human being. The theanthropic sacrifice of the god, into which it is unfortunately impossible for me to enter here as fully as into animal sacrifice, throws a searching retrospective light upon the meaning of the older forms of sacrifice [Smith, 1894, 410 f.]. It confesses, with a frankness that could hardly be excelled, to the fact that the object of the act of sacrifice has always been the same—namely what is now worshipped as God, that is to say, the father. The problem of the relation between animal and human sacrifice thus admits of a simple solution. The original animal sacrifice was already a substitute for a human sacrifice—for the ceremonial killing of the father; so that, when the father-surrogate once more resumed its human shape, the animal sacrifice too could be changed back into a human sacrifice.

The memory of the first great act of sacrifice thus proved indestructible, in spite of every effort to forget it; and at the very point at which men sought to be at the farthest distance from the motives that led to it, its undistorted reproduction emerged in the form of the sacrifice of the god. I need not enlarge here upon the developments of religious thought which, in the shape of rationalizations, made this recurrence possible. Robertson Smith, who had no thought of our derivation of sacrifice from the great event in human prehistory, states that the ceremonies at the festivals in which the ancient Semites celebrated the death of a deity "were currently interpreted as the commemoration of a mythical tragedy " [ibid., 413]. "The mourning," he declares, "is not a spontaneous expression of sympathy with the divine tragedy, but obligatory and enforced by fear of supernatural anger. And a chief object of the mourners is to disclaim responsibility for the god's death—a point which has already come before us in connection with the anthropic sacrifices, such as the 'ox-murder at Athens.'" [Ibid., 412.] It seems most probable that these "current interpretations" were correct and that the feelings of the celebrants were fury explained by the underlying situation.

Let us assume it to be a fact, then, that in the course of the later development of religions the two driving factors, the son's sense of guilt and the son's rebelliousness, never became extinct. Whatever attempt was made at solving the religious problem, whatever kind of reconciliation was effected between these two opposing mental forces, sooner or later broke down under the combined influence, no doubt, of historical events, cultural changes and internal psychical modifications.

The son's efforts to put himself in the place of the father-god became ever more obvious. The introduction of agriculture increased the son's importance in the patriarchal family. He ventured upon new demonstrations of his incestuous libido, which found symbolic satisfaction in his cultivation of Mother Earth. Divine figures such as Attis, Adonis and Tammuz emerged, spirits of vegetation and at the same time youthful divinities enjoying the favours of mother goddesses and committing incest with their mother in defiance of their father. But the sense of guilt, which was not allayed by these creations, found expression in myths which granted only short lives to these youthful favourites of the mother-goddesses and decreed their punishment by emasculation or by the wrath of the father in the form of an animal. Adonis was killed by a wild boar, the sacred animal of Aphrodite; Attis, beloved of Cybele, perished by castration.[11] The mourning for these gods and the rejoicings over their resurrection passed over into the ritual of another son-deity who was destined to lasting success.

When Christianity first penetrated into the ancient world it met with competition from the religion of Mithras and for a time it was doubtful which of the two deities would gain the victory. In spite of the halo of light surrounding his form, the youthful Persian god remains obscure to us. We may perhaps infer from the sculptures of Mithras slaying a bull that he represented a son who was alone in sacrificing his father and thus redeemed his brothers from their burden of complicity in the deed. There was an alternative method of allaying their guilt and this was first adopted by Christ. He sacrificed his own life and so redeemed the company of brothers from original sin.

The doctrine of original sin was of Orphic origin. It formed a part of the mysteries, and spread from them to the schools of philosophy of ancient Greece (Reinach, 1905–12, 2, 75 ff.). Mankind, it was said, were descended from the Titans, who had killed the young Dionysus-Zagreus and had torn him to pieces. The burden of this crime weighed on them. A fragment of Anaximander relates how the unity of the world was broken by a primaeval sin, and that whatever issued from it must bear the punishment. The tumultuous mobbing, the killing and the tearing in pieces by the Titans reminds us clearly enough of the totemic sacrifice described by St. Nilus [ibid., 2, 93]—as, for the matter of that, do many other ancient myths, including, for instance, that of the death of Orpheus himself. Nevertheless, there is a disturbing difference in the fact of the murder having been committed on a *youthful* god.

There can be no doubt that in the Christian myth the original sin was one against God the Father. If, however, Christ redeemed mankind from the burden of original sin by the sacrifice of his own life, we are driven to conclude that the sin was a murder. The law of talion, which is so deeply rooted in human feelings, lays it down that a murder can only be expiated by the sacrifice of another life: self-sacrifice points back to blood-guilt.[12] And if this sacrifice of a life brought about atonement with God the Father, the crime to be expiated can only have been the murder of the father.

In the Christian doctrine therefore, men were acknowledging in the most undisguised manner the guilty primaeval deed, since they found the fullest atonement for it in the sacrifice of this one son. Atonement with the father was all the more complete since the sacrifice was accompanied by a total renunciation of the women on whose account the rebellion against the father was started. But at that point the inexorable psychological law of ambivalence stepped in. The very deed in which the son offered the greatest possible atonement to the father brought him at the same time to the attainment of his wishes *against* the father. He himself became God, beside, or, more correctly, in place of, the father. A son-religion displaced the father-religion. As a sign of this substitution the ancient totem meal was revived in the form of communion, in which the company of brothers consumed the flesh and blood of the son—no longer the father—obtained sanctity thereby and identified themselves with him. Thus we can trace through the ages the identity of the totem meal with animal sacrifice, with theanthropic human sacrifice and with the Christian Eucharist, and we can recognize in all these rituals the effect of the crime by which men were so deeply weighed down but of which they must none the less feel so proud. The Christian communion, however, is essentially a fresh elimination of the father, a repetition of the guilty deed. We can see the full justice of Frazer's pronouncement that "the Christian communion has absorbed within itself a sacrament which is doubtless far older than Christianity."[13]

The Future of an Illusion

While *Totem and Taboo* conjectures about the origins of civilization, *The Future of an Illusion* deals with one of our enduring institutions. It is interesting that even though Freud's subject is an institution, concepts like narcissism and infantile prototype figure prominently in the following excerpt.

In what does the peculiar value of religious ideas lie?

We have spoken of the hostility to civilization which is produced by the pressure that civilization exercises, the renunciations of instinct which it demands. If one imagines its prohibitions lifted—if, then, one may take any woman one pleases as a sexual object, if one may without hesitation kill one's rival for her love or anyone else who stands in one's way, if, too, one can carry off any of the other man's belongings without asking leave—how splendid, what a string of satisfactions one's life would be! True, one soon comes across the first difficulty: everyone else has exactly the same wishes as I have and will treat me with no more consideration than I treat him. And so in reality only one person could be made unrestrictedly happy by such a removal of the restrictions of civilization, and he would be a tyrant, a dictator, who had seized all the means to power. And even he would have every reason to wish that the others would observe at least one cultural commandment: "thou shalt not kill."

But how ungrateful, how short-sighted after all, to strive for the abolition of civilization! What would then remain would be a son of nature, and that would be far harder to bear. It is true that nature would not demand any restrictions of instinct from us, she would let us do as we liked; but she has her own particularly effective method of restricting us. She destroys us—coldly, cruelly, relentlessly, as it seems to us, and possibly through the very things that occasioned our satisfaction. It was precisely because of these dangers with which nature threatens us that we came together

The excerpts in this section are taken from *The Future of an Illusion* by Sigmund Freud, translated by James Strachey. Copyright © 1961 by James Strachey, renewed 1989 by Alix Strachey. Used by permission of W. W. Norton & Company, Inc.

and created civilization, which is also, among other things, intended to make our communal life possible. For the principal task of civilization, its actual *raison d'etre,* is to defend us against nature.

We all know that in many ways civilization does this fairly well already, and clearly as time goes on it will do it much better. But no one is under the illusion that nature has already been vanquished; and few dare hope that she will ever be entirely subjected to man. There are the elements, which seem to mock at all human control: the earth, which quakes and is torn apart and buries all human life and its works; water, which deluges and drowns everything in a turmoil; storms, which blow everything before them; there are diseases, which we have only recently recognized as attacks by other organisms; and finally there is the painful riddle of death, against which no medicine has yet been found, nor probably will be. With these forces nature rises up against us, majestic, cruel and inexorable; she brings to our mind once more our weakness and helplessness, which we thought to escape through the work of civilization. One of the few gratifying and exalting impressions which mankind can offer is when, in the face of an elemental catastrophe, it forgets the discordancies of its civilization and all its internal difficulties and animosities, and recalls the great common task of preserving itself against the superior power of nature.

For the individual, too, life is hard to bear, just as it is for mankind in general. The civilization in which he participates imposes some amount of privation on him, and other men bring him a measure of suffering, either in spite of the precepts of his civilization or because of its imperfections. To this are added the injuries which untamed nature—he calls it Fate—inflicts on him. One might suppose that this condition of things would result in a permanent state of anxious expectation in him and a severe injury to his natural narcissism. We know already how the individual reacts to the injuries which civilization and other men inflict on him: he develops a corresponding degree of resistance to the regulations of civilization and of hostility to it. But how does he defend himself against the superior powers of nature, of Fate, which threaten him as they threaten all the rest?

Civilization relieves him of this task; it performs it in the same way for all alike; and it is noteworthy that in this almost all civilizations act alike. Civilization does not call a halt in the task of defending man against nature, it merely pursues it by other means. The task is a manifold one. Man's self-regard, seriously menaced, calls for consolation; life and the universe must be robbed of their terrors; moreover his curiosity, moved, it is true, by the strongest practical interest, demands an answer.

A great deal is already gained with the first step: the humanization of nature. Impersonal forces and destinies cannot be approached; they remain eternally remote. But if the elements have passions that rage as they do in our own souls, if death itself is not something spontaneous but the violent act of an evil Will, if everywhere in nature there are Beings around us of a kind that we know in our own society, then we can breathe freely, can feel at home in the uncanny and can deal by psychical means with our senseless anxiety. We are still defenceless, perhaps, but we are no longer helplessly paralysed; we can at least react. Perhaps, indeed, we are not even defenceless. We can apply the same methods against these violent supermen outside that we employ in our own society; we can try to adjure them, to appease them, to bribe them, and, by so influencing them, we may rob them of a part of their power. A replacement like this of natural science by psychology not only provides immediate relief, but also points the way to a further mastering of the situation.

For this situation is nothing new. It has an infantile prototype, of which it is in fact only the continuation. For once before one has found oneself in a similar state of helplessness: as a small child, in relation to one's parents. One had reason to fear them, and especially one's father; and yet one was sure of his protection against the dangers one knew. Thus it was natural to assimilate the two situations. Here, too, wishing played its part, as it does in dream-life. The sleeper may be seized with a presentiment of death, which threatens to place him in the grave. But the dream-work knows how to select a condition that will turn even that dreaded event into a wish-fulfilment: the dreamer sees himself in an ancient Etruscan grave which he has climbed down into, happy to find his archaeological interests satisfied. In the same way, a man makes the forces of nature not simply into persons with whom he can associate as he would with his equals—that would not do justice to the overpowering impression which those forces make on him—but he gives them the character of a father. He turns them into gods, following in this, as I have tried to show, not only an infantile prototype but a phylogenetic one.

> The French philosopher Voltaire remarked, "If God did not exist, it would be necessary to create him." Freud contends that religion expresses the individual's and mankind's anxieties, agitations, fears, and expectations. After you read the next excerpt, try to answer this question: Some religions claim that man is God's (religion's) servant. How might Freud view this claim?

In the course of time the first observations were made of regularity and conformity to law in natural phenomena, and with this the forces of nature lost their human traits. But man's helplessness remains and along with it his longing for his father, and the gods. The gods retain their threefold task: they must exorcize the terrors of nature, they must reconcile men to the cruelty of Fate, particularly as it is shown in death, and they must compensate them for the sufferings and privations which a civilized life in common has imposed on them.

But within these functions there is a gradual displacement of accent. It was observed that the phenomena of nature developed automatically according to internal necessities. Without doubt the gods were the lords of nature; they had arranged it to be as it was and now they could leave it to itself. Only occasionally, in what are known as miracles, did they intervene in its course, as though to make it plain that they had relinquished nothing of their original sphere of power. As regards the apportioning of destinies, an unpleasant suspicion persisted that the perplexity and helplessness of the human race could not be remedied. It was here that the gods were most apt to fail. If they themselves created Fate, then their counsels must be deemed inscrutable. The notion dawned on the most gifted people of antiquity that Moira [Fate] stood above the gods and that the gods themselves had their own destinies. And the more autonomous nature became and the more the gods withdrew from it, the more earnestly were all expectations directed to the third function of the gods—the more did morality become their true domain. It now became the task of the gods to even out the defects and evils of civilization, to attend to the sufferings which men inflict on one another in their life together and to watch over the fulfilment of the precepts of civilization, which men obey so imperfectly. Those precepts themselves were credited with a divine origin; they were elevated beyond human society and were extended to nature and the universe.

And thus a store of ideas is created, born from man's need to make his helplessness tolerable and built up from the material of memories of the helplessness of his own childhood and childhood of the human race. It can clearly be seen that the possession of these ideas protects him in two directions—against the dangers of nature and Fate, and against the injuries that threaten him from human society itself. Here is the gist of the matter. Life in this world serves a higher purpose; no doubt it is not easy to guess what that purpose is, but it certainly signifies a perfecting of man's nature. It is probably the spiritual part of man, the soul, which in the course of time has so slowly and unwillingly detached itself from the body, that is the object of this elevation and exaltation. Everything that happens in this world is an expression of the intentions of an intelligence superior to us, which in the end, though its ways and byways are difficult to follow, orders everything for the best—that is, to make it enjoyable for us. Over each one of us there watches a benevolent Providence which is only seemingly stern and which will not suffer us to become a plaything of the over-mighty and pitiless forces of nature. Death itself in not extinction, is not a return to inorganic lifelessness, but the beginning of a new kind of existence which lies on the path of development to something higher. And, looking in the other direction, this view announces that the same moral laws which our civilizations have set up govern the whole universe as well, except that they are maintained by a supreme court of justice with incomparably more power and consistency. In the end all good is rewarded and evil punished, if not actually in this form of life then in the later existences that begin after death. In this way all the terrors, the sufferings and hardships of life are destined to be obliterated. Life after death, which continues life on earth just as the invisible part of the spectrum joins on to the visible part, brings us all the perfection that we may perhaps have missed here. And the superior wisdom which directs this course of things, the infinite goodness that expresses itself in it, the justice that achieves its aim in it—these are the attributes of the divine beings who also created us and the world as a whole, or rather, of the one divine being into which, in our civilization, all the gods of antiquity have been condensed. The people which first succeeded in thus concentrating the divine attributes was not a little proud of the advance. It had laid open to view the father who had all along been hidden behind every divine figure as its nucleus. Fundamentally this was a return to the historical beginnings of the idea of God. Now that God was a single person, man's relations to him could recover the intimacy and intensity of the child's relation to his father. But if one had done so much for one's father, one wanted to have a reward, or at least to be his only beloved child, his Chosen People. Very much later, pious America laid claim to being "God's own Country"; and, as regards one of the shapes in which men worship the deity, the claim is undoubtedly valid.

The religious ideas that have been summarized above have of course passed through a long process of development and have been adhered to in various phases by various civilizations. I have singled out one such phase, which roughly corresponds to the final form taken by our present day white Christian civilization. It is easy to see that not all the parts of this picture tally equally well with one another, that not all the questions that press for an answer receive one, and that it is difficult to dismiss the contradiction of daily experience. Nevertheless, such as they are, those ideas—ideas which are religious in the widest sense—are prized as the most precious possession of civilization, as the most precious thing it has to offer its participants. It is far more highly prized than all the devices for winning treasures from the earth or providing men with sustenance or preventing their illnesses, and so forth. People feel that life would not be tolerable if they did not attach to these ideas the value that is claimed for them. And now the question arises: what are these ideas in the light of psychology? Whence do they derive the esteem in which they are held? And, to take a further timid step, what is their real worth?

Group Psychology and the Analysis of the Ego

If the first principle of group psychology is the individual's lack of freedom, why does Freud suggest that eros (erotic love) and libido (emotional ties) play essential roles in maintaining groups?

I shall make an attempt at using the concept of libido for the purpose of throwing light upon group psychology, a concept which has done us such good service in the study of psychoneuroses.

Libido is an expression taken from the theory of the emotions. We call by that name the energy, regarded as a quantitative magnitude (though not at present actually measurable), of those instincts which have to do with all that may be comprised under the word "love." The nucleus of what we mean by love naturally consists (and this is what is commonly called love, and what the poets sing of) in sexual love with sexual union as its aim. But we do not separate from this—what in any case has a share in the name "love"—on the one hand, self-love, and on the other, love for parents and children, friendship and love for humanity in general, and also devotion to concrete objects and to abstract ideas. Our justification lies in the fact that psycho-analytic research has taught us that all these tendencies are an expression of the same instinctual impulses; in relations between the sexes these impulses force their way towards sexual union, but in other circumstances they are diverted from this aim or are prevented from reaching it, though always preserving enough of their original nature to keep their identity recognizable (as in such features as the longing for proximity, and self-sacrifice).

We are of opinion, then, that language has carried out an entirely justifiable piece of unification in creating the word "love" with its numerous uses, and that we cannot do better than take it as the basis of our scientific discussions and expositions as well. By coming to this decision, psycho-analysis has let loose a storm of indignation, as though it had been guilty of an act of outrageous innovation. Yet it has done nothing original in taking love in this "wider" sense. In its origin, function, and relation to sexual love, the "Eros" of the philosopher Plato coincides exactly with the love-force, the libido of psycho-analysis, as has been shown in detail by Nachmansohn (1915) and Pfister (1921); and when the apostle Paul, in his famous epistle to the Corinthians, praises love above all else, he certainly understands it in the same "wider" sense. But this only shows that men do not always take their great thinkers seriously, even when they profess most to admire them.

Psycho-analysis, then, gives these love instincts the name of sexual instincts, *a potiori* and by reason of their origin. The majority of "educated" people have regarded this nomenclature as an insult, and have taken their revenge by retorting upon psycho-analysis with the reproach of "pan-sexualism." Anyone who considers sex as something mortifying and humiliating to human nature is at liberty to make use of the more genteel expressions "Eros" and "erotic." I might have done so myself from the first and thus have spared myself much opposition. But I did not want to, for I like to avoid concessions to faintheartedness. One can never tell where that road may lead one; one gives way first in words, and then little by little in substance too. I cannot see any merit in being ashamed of sex; the Greek word "Eros," which is to soften the affront, is in the end nothing more than a translation of our German word *Liebe* [love]; and finally, he who knows how to wait need make no concessions.

We will try our fortune, then, with the supposition that love relationships (or, to use a more neutral expression, emotional ties) also constitute the essence of the group mind. Let us remember that the authorities make no mention of any such relations. What would correspond to them is evidently concealed behind the shelter, the screen, of suggestion. Our hypothesis finds support in the first instance from two passing thoughts. First, that a group is clearly held together by a power of some kind: and to what power could this feat be better ascribed than to Eros,[1] which holds together everything in the world? Secondly, that if an individual gives up his distinctiveness in a group and lets its other members influence him by suggestion, it gives one the impression that he does it because he feels the need of being in harmony with them rather than in opposition to them—so that perhaps after all he does it "*ihnen zu Liebe.*"[2] . . .

A Church and an army are artificial groups—that is, a certain external force is employed to prevent them from disintegrating[3] and to check alterations in their structure. As a rule a person is not consulted, or is given no choice, as to whether he wants to enter such a group; any attempt at leaving it is usually met with persecution or with severe punishment, or has quite definite conditions attached to it. It is quite outside our present interest to enquire why these associations need such special safeguards. We are only attracted by one circumstance, namely that certain facts, which are far more concealed in other cases, can be observed very clearly in those highly organized groups which are protected from dissolution in the manner that has been mentioned.

In a Church (and we may with advantage take the Catholic Church as a type) as well as in an army, however different the two may be in other respects, the same illusion holds good of there being a head—in the Catholic Church Christ, in an army its Commander-in-Chief—who loves all the individuals in the group with an equal love. Everything depends upon this illusion; if it were to be dropped, then both Church and army would dissolve, so far as the external force permitted them to. This equal love was expressly enunciated by Christ: "Inasmuch as ye have done it unto one of the least of these my brethren, ye have done it unto me." He stands to the individual members of the group of believers in the relation of a kind elder brother; he is their substitute father. All the demands that are made upon the individual are derived from this love of Christ's. A democratic strain runs through the Church, for the very reason that before Christ everyone is equal, and that everyone has an equal share in his love. It is not without a deep reason that the similarity between the Christian community and a family is invoked, and that believers call themselves brothers in Christ, that is, brothers through the love which Christ has for them. There is no doubt that the tie which unites each individual with Christ is also the cause of the tie which unites them one another. The like holds good of an army. The Commander-in-Chief is a father who loves all soldiers equally, and for that reason they are comrades among themselves. The army differs structurally from the Church in being built up of a series of such groups. Every captain is, as it were, the Commander-in-Chief and the father of his company, and so is every non-commissioned officer of his section. It is true that a similar hierarchy has been constructed in the Church, but it does not play the same part in it economically[4]; for more knowledge and care about individuals may be attributed to Christ than to a human Commander-in-Chief.

An objection will justly be raised against this conception of the libidal structure of an army on the ground that no place has been found in it for such ideas as those of one's country, of national glory, etc., which are of such importance in holding an army together. The answer is that that is a different instance of a group tie, and no longer such a simple one; for the examples of great generals, like Caeser, Wallenstein, or Napoleon, show that such ideas are not indispensable to the existence of an army. We shall presently touch upon the possibility of a leading idea being substituted for a leader and upon the relations between the two. The neglect of this libidinal factor in an army, even when it is not the only factor operative, seems to be not merely a theoretical omission but also a practical danger. Prussian militarism, which was just as unpsychological as German science, may have had to suffer the consequences of this in the [first] World War. We know that the war neuroses which ravaged the German army have been recognized as being a protest of the individual against the part he was expected to play in the army; and according to the communication of Simmel (1918), the hard treatment of the men by their superiors may be considered as foremost among the motive forces of the disease. . . .

It is to be noticed that in these two artificial groups each individual is bound by libidinal ties on the one hand to the leader (Christ, the Commander-in-Chief) and on the other hand to the other members of the group. How these two ties are related to each other, whether they are of the same kind and the same value, and how they are to be described psychologically—these questions must be reserved for subsequent enquiry. But we shall venture even now upon a mild reproach against earlier writers for not having sufficiently appreciated the importance of the leader in the psychology of the group, while our own choice of this as a first subject for investigation has brought us into a more favourable position. It would appear as though we were on the right road towards an explanation of the principal phenomenon of group psychology—the individual's lack of freedom in a group. If each individual is bound in two directions by such an intense emotional tie, we shall find no difficulty in attributing to that circumstance the alteration and limitation which have been observed in his personality.

> The next passage is concerned with the dissolution of groups and group behavior, yet Freud makes a puzzling statement about the tendency for religions to be harsh and cruel toward unbelievers. Why does he say that this phenomenon, of which history provides many examples, *must* occur?

A hint to the same effect, that the essence of a group lies in the libidinal ties existing in it, is also to be found in the phenomenon of panic, which is best studied in military groups. A panic arises if a group of that kind becomes disintegrated. Its characteristics are that none of the orders given by superiors are any longer listened to, and that each individual is only solicitous on his own account, and without any consideration for the rest. The mutual ties have ceased to exist, and a gigantic and senseless fear is set free. At this point, again, the objection will naturally be made that it is rather the other way round; and that the fear has grown so great as to be able to disregard all ties and all feelings of consideration for others. McDougall [1920, 24] has even made use of panic (though not of military panic) as a typical instance of that intensification of emotion by contagion ("primary induction") on which he lays so much emphasis. But nevertheless this rational method of explanation is here quite inadequate. The very question that needs explanation is why the fear has become so gigantic. The greatness of the danger cannot be responsible, for the same army which now falls a victim to panic may previously have faced equally great or greater danger with complete success; it is of the very essence of panic that it bears no relation to the danger that threatens, and often breaks out on the most trivial occasions. If an individual in panic fear begins to be solicitous only on his own account, he bears witness in so doing to the fact that the emotional ties, which have hitherto made the danger seem small to him, have ceased to exist. Now that he is by himself in facing the danger, he may surely think it greater. The fact is, therefore, that panic fear presupposes a relaxation in the libidinal structure of the group and reacts to that relaxation in a justifiable manner, and the contrary view—that the libidinal ties of the group are destroyed owing to fear in the face of the danger—can be refuted.

The contention that fear in a group is increased to enormous proportions through induction (contagion) is not in the least contradicted by these remarks. McDougall's view meets the case entirely when the danger is a really great one and when the group has no strong emotional ties—conditions which are fulfilled, for instance, when a fire breaks out in a theatre or a place of amusement. But the truly instructive case and the one which can be best employed for our purposes is that mentioned above, in which a body of troops breaks into a panic although the danger has not increased beyond a degree that is usual and has often been previously faced. It is not to be expected that the usage of the word "panic" should be clearly and unambiguously determined. Sometimes it is used to describe any collective fear, sometimes even fear in an individual when it exceeds all bounds, and often the name seems to be reserved for cases in which the outbreak of fear is not warranted by the occasion. If we take the word "panic" in the sense of collective fear, we can establish a far-reaching analogy. Fear in an individual is provoked either by the greatness of a danger or by the cessation of emotional ties (libidinal cathexes); the latter is the case of neurotic fear or anxiety. In just the same way panic arises either owing to an increase of the common danger or owing to the disappearance of the emotional ties which hold the group together; and the latter case is analogous to that of neurotic anxiety.

Anyone who, like McDougall [1920], describes a panic as one of the plainest functions of the "group mind," arrives at the paradoxical position that this group mind does away with itself in one of its most striking manifestations. It is impossible to doubt that panic means the disintegration of a group; it involves the cessation of all the feelings of consideration which the members of the group otherwise show one another.

The typical occasion of the outbreak of a panic is very much as it is represented in Nestray's parody of Hebbel's play about Judith and Holofernes. A soldier cries out: "The general has lost his head!" and thereupon all the Assyrians take to flight. The loss of the leader in some sense or other, the birth of misgivings about him, brings on the outbreak of panic, though the danger remains the same; the mutual ties between the members of the group disappear, as a rule, at the same time as the tie with their leader. The group vanishes in dust. . . .

The dissolution of a religious group is not so easy to observe. A short time ago there came into my hands an English novel of Catholic origin, recommended by the Bishop of London, with the title *When It Was Dark*. It gave a clever and, as it seems to me, a convincing picture of such a possibility and its consequences. The novel, which is supposed to relate to the present day, tells how a conspiracy of enemies of the person of Christ and of the Christian Faith succeed in arranging for a sepulcher to be discovered in Jerusalem. In this sepulcher is an inscription, in which Joseph of Arimathaea confesses that for reasons of piety he secretly removed the body of Christ from its grave on the third day after its entombment and buried it in this spot. The resurrecting of Christ and his divine nature are by this means disproved, and the result of this archaeological discovery is a convulsion in European civilization and an extraordinary increase in all crimes and acts of alliance which only ceases when the forgers' plot has been revealed.

The phenomenon which accompanies the dissolution that is here supposed to overtake a religious group is not fear, for which the occasion is wanting. Instead of it ruthless and hostile impulses towards other people make their appearance, which, owing to the equal love of Christ, they had previously been unable to do. But even during the kingdom of Christ those people who do not belong to the community of believers, who do not love him, and whom he does not love, stand outside this tie. Therefore a religion, even if it calls itself the religion of love, must be hard and unloving to those who do not belong to it. Fundamentally indeed every religion is in this same way a religion of love for all those whom it embraces; while cruelty and intolerance towards those who do not belong to it are natural to every religion. However difficult we may find it personally, we ought not to reproach believers too severely on this account; people who are unbelieving or indifferent are much better off psychologically in this matter [of cruelty and intolerance]. If to-day that intolerance no longer shows itself so violent and cruel as in former centuries, we can scarcely conclude that there has been a softening in human manners. The cause is rather to be found in the undeniable weakening of religious feelings and the libidinal ties which depend upon them. If another group tie takes the place of the religious one—and the socialistic tie seems to be succeeding in doing so—then there will be the same intolerance towards outsiders as in the age of the Wars of Religion; and if differences between scientific opinions could ever attain a similar significance for groups, the same result would again be repeated with this new motivation.

> A curious thing occurs when individuals join a group: their inherent self-love (narcissism), which makes enemies of others, decreases and the individual begins to love the other group members. After reading the next excerpt, try to answer the following question: Do you think that the love that members of a group feel for each other increases or decreases the group's hostility or intolerance toward non-members?

Let us keep before our eyes the nature of the emotional relations which hold between men in general. According to Schopenhauer's famous simile of the freezing porcupines no one can tolerate a too intimate approach to his neighbor.[5]

The evidence of psycho-analysis shows that almost every intimate emotional relation between two people which lasts for some time—marriage, friendship, the relations between parents and children[6]—leaves a sediment of feeling of aversion and hostility, which only escapes perception as a result of repression. This is less disguised in the common wrangles between business partners or in the grumbles of a subordinate at his superior. The same thing happens when men come together in larger units. Every time two families become connected by a marriage each of them thinks itself superior to or of better birth than the other. Of two neighboring towns each is the other's most jealous rival; every little canton looks down upon the others with contempt. Closely related races keep one another at arm's length; the South German cannot endure the North German, the Englishman casts every kind of aspersion upon the Scot, the Spaniard despises the Portuguese. We are no longer astonished that greater differences should lead to an almost insuperable repugnance, such as the Gallic people feel for the German, the Aryan for the Semite, and the white races for the coloured.

When this hostility is directed against people who are otherwise loved we describe it as ambivalence of feeling; and we explain the fact, in what is probably far too rational a manner, by means of the numerous occasions for conflicts of interest which arise precisely in such intimate relations. In the undisguised antipathies and aversions which people feel towards strangers with whom they have to do we may recognize the expression of self-love—of narcissism. This self-love works for the preservation of the individual, and behaves as though the occurrence of any divergence from his own particular lines of development involved a criticism of them and a demand for their alteration. We do not know why such sensitiveness should have been directed to just these details of differentiation; but it is unmistakable that in this whole connection men give evidence of a readiness for hatred, an aggressiveness, the source of which is unknown, and to which one is tempted to ascribe an elementary character.[7]

But when a group is formed the whole of this intolerance vanishes, temporarily or permanently, within the group. So long as a group formation persists or so far as it extends, individuals in the group behave as though they were uniform, tolerate the peculiarities of its other members, equate themselves with them, and have no feeling of aversion towards them. Such a limitation of narcissism can, according to our theoretical views, only be produced by one factor, a libidinal tie with other people. Love for oneself knows only one barrier—love for others, love for objects. The question will at once be raised whether community of interest in itself, without any addition of libido, must not necessarily lead to the toleration of other people and to considerateness for them. This objection may be met by the reply that nevertheless no lasting limitation of narcissism is effected in this way, since this tolerance does not persist longer than the immediate advantage gained from the other people's collaboration. But the practical importance of this discussion is less than might be supposed, for experience has shown that in cases of collaboration libidinal ties are regularly formed between the fellow-workers which prolong and solidify the relation between them to a point beyond what is merely profitable. The same thing occurs in men's social relations as has become familiar to psycho-analytic research in the course of the development of the individual libido. The libido attaches itself to the satisfaction of the great vital needs, and chooses as its first objects the people who have a share in that process. And in the development of mankind as a whole, just as in individuals, love alone acts as the civilizing factor in the sense that it brings a change from egoism to altruism. And this is true both of sexual love for women, with all the obligations which it involves of not harming the things that are dear to women, and also of desexualized, sublimated homosexual love for other men, which springs from work in common.

If therefore in groups narcissistic self-love is subject to limitations which do not operate outside them, that is cogent evidence that the essence of a group formation consists in new kinds of libidinal ties among the members of the group.

> Since an individual's entry into a group requires so much sacrifice of her or his individuality, the popularity of groups seems puzzling. Freud implies that groups are not solely imposed on the individual but also appeal to individual needs and desires. Why *are* groups so popular?

It might be said that the intense emotional ties which we observe in groups are quite sufficient to explain one of their characteristics—the lack of independence and initiative in their members, the similarity in the reactions of all of them, their reduction, so to speak, to the level of group individuals. But if we look at it as a whole, a group shows us more than this. Some of its features—the weakness of intellectual ability, the lack of emotional restraint, the incapacity for moderation and delay, the inclination to exceed every limit in the expression of emotion and to work it off completely in the form of action—these and similar features, which we find so impressively described in Le Bon, show an unmistakable picture of a regression of mental activity to an earlier stage such as we are not surprised to find among savages or children. A regression of this sort is in particular an essential characteristic of common groups, while, as we have heard, in organized and artificial groups it can to a large extent be checked.

We thus have an impression of a state in which an individual's private emotional impulses and intellectual acts are too weak to come to anything by themselves and are entirely dependent for this on being reinforced by being repeated in a similar way in the other members of the group. We are reminded of how many of these phenomena of dependence are part of the normal constitution of human society, of how little originality and personal courage are to be found in it, of how much every individual is ruled by those attitudes of the group mind which exhibit themselves in such forms as racial characteristics, class prejudices, public opinion, etc.

Civilization and Its Discontents

Civilization and Its Discontents is Freud's most comprehensive analysis of culture. When considering the following passages, think about this statement: This is not the life we would freely choose, and the large percentage of Americans addicted to nicotine, caffeine, alcohol, drugs, exercise, or something other proves the point.

The question of the purpose of human life has been raised countless times; it has never yet received a satisfactory answer and perhaps does not admit of one. Some of those who have asked it have added that if it should turn out that life has no purpose, it would lose all value for them. But this threat alters nothing. It looks, on the contrary, as though one had a right to dismiss the question, for it seems to derive from the human presumptuousness, many other manifestations of which are already familiar to us. Nobody talks about the purpose of the life of animals, unless, perhaps, it may be supposed to lie in being of service to man. But this view is not tenable either, for there are many animals of which man can make nothing, except to describe, classify and study them; and innumerable species of animals have escaped even this use, since they existed and became extinct before man set eyes on them. Once again, only religion can answer the question of the purpose of life. One can hardly be wrong in concluding that the idea of life having a purpose stands and falls with the religious system.

We will therefore turn to the less ambitious question of what men themselves show by their behaviour to be the purpose and intention of their lives. What do they demand of life and wish to achieve in it? The answer to this can hardly be in doubt. They strive after happiness; they want to become happy and to remain so. This endeavour has two sides, a positive and a negative aim. It aims, on the one hand, at an absence of pain and unpleasure, and, on the other, at the experiencing of strong feelings of pleasure. In its narrower sense the word "happiness" only relates to the last. In conformity with

The excerpts in this section are taken from *Civilization and Its Discontents* by Sigmund Freud, translated by James Strachey. Copyright © 1961 by James Strachey; renewed 1989 by Alix Strachey. Used by permission of W. W. Norton & Company, Inc.

this dichotomy in his aims, man's activity develops in two directions, according as it seeks to realize—in the main, or even exclusively—the one or the other of these aims.

As we see, what decides the purpose of life is simply the programme of the pleasure principle. This principle dominates the operation of the mental apparatus from the start. There can be no doubt about its efficacy, and yet its programme is at loggerheads with the whole world, with the macrocosm as much as with the microcosm. There is no possibility at all of its being carried through; all the regulations of the universe run counter to it. One feels inclined to say that the intention that man should be "happy" is not included in the plan of "Creation." What we call happiness in the strictest sense comes from the (preferably sudden) satisfaction of needs which have been dammed up to a high degree, and it is from its nature only possible as an episodic phenomenon. When any situation that is desired by the pleasure principle is prolonged, it only produces a feeling of mild contentment. We are so made that we can derive intense enjoyment only from a contrast and very little from a state of things.[1] Thus our possibilities of happiness are already restricted by our constitution. Unhappiness is much less difficult to experience. We are threatened with suffering from three directions: from our own body, which is doomed to decay and dissolution and which cannot even do without pain and anxiety as warning signals; from the external world, which may rage against us with overwhelming and merciless forces of destruction; and finally from our relations to other men. The suffering which comes from this last source is perhaps more painful to us than any other. We tend to regard it as a kind of gratuitous addition although it cannot be any less fatefully inevitable than the suffering which comes from elsewhere.

It is no wonder if, under the pressure of these possibilities of suffering, men are accustomed to moderate their claims to happiness—just as the pleasure principle itself, indeed, under the influence of the external world, changed into the more modest reality principle—if a man thinks himself happy merely to have escaped unhappiness or to have survived his suffering, and if in general the task of avoiding suffering pushes that of obtaining pleasure into the background. Reflection shows that the accomplishment of this task can be attempted along very different paths; and all these paths have been recommended by the various schools of worldly wisdom and put into practice by men. An unrestricted satisfaction of every need presents itself as the most enticing method of conducting one's life, but it means putting enjoyment before caution, and soon brings its own punishment. The other methods, in which avoidance of unpleasure is the main purpose, are differentiated according to the source of unpleasure to which their attention is chiefly turned. Same of these methods are extreme and some moderate; some are one-sided and some attack the problem simultaneously at several points. Against the suffering which may come upon one from human relationships the readiest safeguard is voluntary isolation, keeping oneself aloof from other people. The happiness which can be achieved along this path is, as we see, the happiness of quietness. Against the dreaded external world one can only defend oneself by some kind of turning away from it, if one intends to solve the task by oneself. There is, indeed, another and better path: that of becoming a member of the human community, and, with the help of a technique guided by science, going over to the attack against nature and subjecting her to the human will. Then one is working with all for the good of all. But the most interesting methods of averting suffering are those which seek to influence our own organism. In the last analysis, all suffering is nothing else than sensation; it only exists in so far as we feel it, and we only feel it in consequence of certain ways in which our organism is regulated.

The crudest, but also the most effective among these methods of influence is the chemical one—intoxication. I do not think that anyone completely understands its mechanism, but it is a fact that there are foreign substances which, when present in the blood or tissues, directly cause us pleasurable sensations; and they also so alter the conditions governing our sensibility that we become incapable of receiving unpleasurable impulses. The two effects not only occur simultaneously, but seem to be intimately bound up with each other. But there must be substances in the chemistry of our own bodies which have similar effects, for we know at least one pathological state, mania, in which a condition similar to intoxication arises without the administration of any intoxicating drug. Besides this, our normal mental life exhibits oscillations between a comparatively easy liberation of pleasure and a comparatively difficult one, parallel with which there goes a diminished or an increased receptivity to unpleasure. It is greatly to be regretted that this toxic side of mental processes has so far escaped scientific examination. The service rendered by intoxicating media in the struggle for happiness and in keeping misery at a distance is so highly prized as a benefit that individuals and peoples alike have given them an established place in the economics of their libido. We owe to such media not merely the immediate yield of pleasure, but also a greatly desired degree of independence from the external world. For one knows that, with the help of this "drowner of cares" one can at any time withdraw from the pressure of reality and find refuge in a world of one's own with better conditions of sensibility. As is well known, it is precisely this property of intoxicants which also determines their danger and their injuriousness. They are responsible, in certain circumstances, for the useless waste of a large quota of energy which might have been employed for the improvement of the human lot.

> If humans seek happiness, why do we create a civilized life when such a life requires so many restrictions? But our civil societies have often not been so civil. Would we be happier in a state of nature?

Our enquiry concerning happiness has not so far taught us much that is not already common knowledge. And even if we proceed from it to the problem of why it is hard for men to be happy, there seems no greater prospect of learning anything new. We have given the answer already[2] . . . by pointing to the three sources from which our suffering comes: the superior power of nature, the feebleness of our own bodies and the inadequacy of the regulations which adjust the mutual relationships of human beings in the family, the state and society. In regard to the first two sources, our judgement cannot hesitate long. It forces us to acknowledge those sources of suffering and to submit to the inevitable. We shall never completely master nature; and our bodily organism, itself a part of that nature, will always remain a transient structure with a limited capacity for adaptation and achievement. This recognition does not have a paralysing effect. On the contrary, it points the direction for our activity. If we cannot remove all suffering, we can remove some, and we can mitigate some: the experience of many thousands of years has convinced us of that. As regards the third source, the social source of suffering, our attitude is a different one. We do not admit it at all; we cannot see why the regulations made by ourselves should not, on the contrary, be a protection and a benefit for every one of us. And yet, when we consider how unsuccessful we have been in precisely this field of prevention of suffering a suspicion dawns on us that here, too, a piece of unconquerable nature may lie behind—this time a piece of our own psychical constitution.

When we start considering this possibility, we come upon a contention which is so astonishing that we must dwell upon it. This contention holds that what we call our civilization is largely responsible for our misery, and that we should be much happier if we gave it up and returned to primitive conditions. I call this contention astonishing because, in whatever way we may define the concept of civilization, it is a certain fact that all the things with which we seek to protect ourselves against the threats that emanate from the sources of suffering are part of that very civilization.

> The development of civilized life requires that most of our instincts "go into hiding," but those instincts eventually reveal themselves or want to. However, if we are both individuals and members of a community, we should not find this irony so puzzling.

Beauty, cleanliness and order obviously occupy a special position among the requirements of civilization. No one will maintain that they are as important for life as control over the forces of nature or as some other factors with which we shall become acquainted. And yet no one would care to put them in the background as trivialities. That civilization is not exclusively taken up with what is useful is already shown by the example of beauty, which we decline to omit from among the interests of civilization. The usefulness of order is quite evident. With regard to cleanliness, we must bear in mind that it is demanded of us by hygiene as well, and we may suspect that even before the days of scientific prophylaxis the connection between the two was not altogether strange to man. Yet utility does not entirely explain these efforts; something else must be at work besides.

No feature, however, seems better to characterize civilization than its esteem and encouragement of man's higher mental activities—his intellectual, scientific and artistic achievements—and the leading role that it assigns to ideas in human life. Foremost among those ideas are the religious systems, on whose complicated structure I have endeavoured to throw light elsewhere. Next come the speculations of philosophy; and finally what might be called man's "ideals"—his ideas of a possible perfection of individuals or of peoples or of the whole of humanity and the demands he sets up on the basis of such ideas. The fact that these creations of his are not independent of one another, but are on the contrary closely interwoven, increases the difficulty not only of describing them but of tracing their psychological derivation. If we assume quite generally that the motive force of all human activities is a striving towards the two confluent goals of utility and a yield of pleasure, we must suppose that this is also true of the manifestations of civilization which we have been discussing here, although this is easily visible only in scientific and aesthetic activities. But it cannot be doubted that the other activities, too, correspond to strong needs in men—perhaps to needs which are only developed in a minority. Nor must we allow ourselves to be misled by judgements of value concerning any particular religion, or philosophic system, or ideal. Whether we think to find in them the highest achievements of the human spirit, or whether we deplore them as aberrations, we cannot but recognize that where they are present, and, in especial, where they are dominant, a high level of civilization is implied.

The last, but certainly not the least important, of the characteristic features of civilization remains to be assessed: the manner in which the relationships of men to one another, their social relationships, are regulated—relationships which affect a person as a neighbor, as a source of help, as another person's sexual object, as a member of a family and of a State. Here it is especially difficult to keep clear of particular ideal demands and to see what is civilized in general. Perhaps we may begin by explaining that the element of civilization enters on the scene with the first attempt to regulate these social relationships. If the attempt were not made, the relationships would be subject to the arbitrary will of the individual: that is to say, the physically stronger man would decide them in the sense of his own interests and instinctual impulses. Nothing would be changed in this if this stronger man should in his turn meet someone even stronger than he. Human life in common is only made possible when a majority comes together which is stronger than any separate individual and which remains united against all separate individuals. The power of this community is then set up as "right" in opposition to the power of the individual, which is condemned as "brute force." This replacement of the power of the individual by the power of a community constitutes the decisive step of civilization. The essence of it lies in the fact that the members of the community restrict themselves in their possibilities of satisfaction, whereas the individual knew no such restrictions. The first requisite of civilization, therefore, is that of justice—that is, the assurance that a law once made will not be broken in favour of an individual. This implies nothing as to the ethical value of such a law. The further course of cultural development seems to tend towards making the law no longer an expression of the will of a small community—a caste or a stratum of the population or a racial group—which, in its turn, behaves like a violent individual towards other, and perhaps more numerous, collections of people. The final outcome should be a rule of law to which all—except those who are not capable of entering a community—have contributed by a sacrifice of their instincts, and which leaves no one—again with the same exception—at the mercy of brute force.

The liberty of the individual is no gift of civilization. It was greatest before there was any civilization, though then, it is true, it had for the most part no value, since the individual was scarcely in a position to defend it. The development of civilization imposes restrictions on it, and justice demands that no one shall escape those restrictions. What makes itself felt in a human community as a desire for freedom may be their revolt against some existing injustice, and so may prove favourable to a further development of civilization; it may remain compatible with civilization. But it may also spring from the remains of their original personality, which is still untamed by civilization and may thus become the basis in them of hostility to civilization. The urge for freedom, therefore, is directed against particular forms and demands of civilization or against civilization altogether. It does not seem as though any influence could induce a man to change his nature into a termite's. No doubt he will always defend his claim to individual liberty against the will of the group. A good part of the struggles of mankind centre round the single task of finding an expedient accommodation—one, that is, that will bring happiness—between this claim of the individual and the cultural claims of the group; and one of the problems that touches the fate of humanity is whether such an accommodation can be reached by means of some particular form of civilization or whether this conflict is irreconcilable.

> Freud's implicit doubts regarding Enlightenment optimism burn brightly in his thoughts on communism; however, he asks a crucial question—will cultural development succeed, in the long run, in defeating human aggression?

The existence of this inclination to aggression, which we can detect in ourselves and justly assume to be present in others, is the factor which disturbs our relations with our neighbour and which forces civilization into such a high expenditure [of energy]. In consequence of this primary mutual hostility of human beings, civilized society is perpetually threatened with disintegration. The interest of work in common would not hold it together; instinctual passions are stronger than reasonable interests. Civilization has to use its utmost efforts in order to set limits to man's aggressive instincts and to hold the manifestations of them in check by psychical reaction-formations. Hence, therefore, the use of methods intended to incite people into identifications and aim-inhibited relationships of love, hence the restriction upon sexual life, and hence too the ideal's commandment to love one's neighbour as oneself—a commandment which is really justified by the fact that nothing else runs so strongly counter to the original nature of man. In spite of every effort, these endeavors of civilization have not so far achieved very much. It hopes to prevent the crudest excesses of brutal violence by itself assuming the right to use violence against criminals, but the law is not able to lay hold of the more cautious and refined manifestations of human aggressiveness. The time comes when each one of us has to give up as illusions the expectations which, in his youth, he pinned upon his fellow-men, and when he may learn how much difficulty and pain has been added to his life by their ill-will. At the same time, it would be unfair to reproach civilization with trying to eliminate strife and competition from human activity. These things are undoubtedly indispensable. But opposition is not necessarily enmity; it is merely misused and made an *occasion* for enmity.

The communists believe that they have found the path to deliverance from our evils. According to them, man is wholly good and is well-disposed to his neighbour; but the institution of private property has corrupted his nature. The ownership of private wealth gives the individual power, and with it the temptation to ill-treat his neighbor; while the man who is excluded from possession is bound to rebel in hostility against his oppressor. If private property were abolished, all wealth held in common, and everyone allowed to share in the enjoyment of it, ill-will and hostility would disappear among men. Since everyone's needs would be satisfied, no one would have any reason to regard another as his enemy; all would willingly undertake the work that was necessary. I have no concern with any economic criticisms of the communist system; I cannot enquire into whether the abolition of private property is expedient or advantageous.[3] But I am able to recognize that the psychological premises on which the system is based are an untenable illusion. In abolishing private property we deprive the human love of aggression of one of its instruments, certainly a strong one, though certainly not the strongest; but we have in no way altered the differences in power and influence which are misused by aggressiveness, nor have we altered anything in its nature. Aggressiveness was not created by property. It reigned almost without limit in primitive times, when property was still very scanty, and it already shows itself in the nursery almost before property has given up its primal, anal form; it forms the basis of every relation of affection and love among people (with the single exception, perhaps, of the mother's relation to her male child). If we do away with personal rights over material wealth, there still remains prerogative in the field of sexual relationships, which is bound to become the source of the strongest dislike and the most violent hostility among men who in other respects are on an equal footing. If we were to remove this factor, too, by allowing complete freedom of sexual life and thus abolishing the family, the germ-cell of civilization, we cannot, it is true, easily foresee what new paths the development of civilization could take; but one thing we can expect, and that is that this indestructible feature of human nature will follow it there.

It is clearly not easy for men to give up the satisfaction of this inclination to aggression. They do not feel comfortable without it. The advantage which a comparatively small cultural group offers of allowing this instinct an outlet in the form of hostility against intruders is not to be despised. It is always possible to bind together a considerable number of people in love, so long as there are other people left over to receive the manifestations of their aggressiveness. I once discussed the phenomenon that it is precisely communities with adjoining territories, and related to each other in other ways as well, who are engaged in constant feuds and in ridiculing each other—like the Spaniards and Portuguese, for instance, the North Germans and South Germans, the English and Scotch, and so on. I gave this phenomenon the name of "the narcissism of minor differences," a name which does not do much to explain it. We can now see that it is a convenient and relatively harmless satisfaction of the inclination to aggression, by means of which cohesion between the members of the community is made easier. In this respect the Jewish people, scattered everywhere, have rendered most useful services to the civilizations of the countries that have been their hosts;

but unfortunately all the massacres of the Jews in the Middle Ages did not suffice to make that period more peaceful and secure for their Christian fellows. When once the Apostle Paul had posited universal love between men as the foundation of the Christian community, extreme intolerance on the part of Christendom towards those who remained outside it became the inevitable consequence. To the Romans, who had not founded their communal life as a State upon love, religious intolerance was something foreign, although with them religion was a concern of the State and the State was permeated by religion. Neither was it an unaccountable chance that the dream of a Germanic world-dominion called for anti-Semitism as its complement; and it is intelligible that the attempt to establish a new, communist civilization in Russia should find its psychological support in the persecution of the bourgeois. One only wonders, with concern, what the Soviets will do after they have wiped out their bourgeois. . . .

The fateful question for the human species seems to me to be whether and to what extent their cultural development will succeed in mastering the disturbance of their communal life by the human instinct of aggression and self-destruction. It may be that in this respect precisely the present time deserves a special interest. Men have gained control over the forces of nature to such an extent that with their help they would have no difficulty in exterminating one another to the last man. They know this, and hence comes a large part of their current unrest, their unhappiness and their mood of anxiety. And now it is to be expected that the other of the two "Heavenly Powers," eternal Eros, will make an effort to assert himself in the struggle with his equally immortal adversary. But who can foresee with what success and with what result?

Part Three

Master Passages: Freud's Observations on Psychoanalysis and Its Uses

The observations that follow are short quotations from a number of Freud's works more fully excerpted in this text. Publication information for each source is provided in the corresponding chapter of this book; the numbers in parentheses after each quotation indicate the page numbers in the source.

Psychoanalysis created a lens by which to view humans, society, and their conflicts. The following quotes could be called "master passages" since they represent major Freudian concepts. These excerpts are useful starting places for review, and if you can explain them accurately you will have mastered *Uncovering Our Masks.*

The Development of Psychoanalysis

An Autobiographical Study

"I received the profoundest impression of the possibility that there could be powerful mental processes which nevertheless remained hidden from the consciousness of men." (17)

"I now learned from my rapidly increasing experience that it was not any kind of emotional excitation that was in action behind the phenomena of neurosis but habitually one of a sexual nature." (23)

"How had it come about that the patients had forgotten so many of the facts of their external and internal lives. Everything that had been forgotten had in some way . . . been distressing." (29)

Introductory Lectures on Psycho-Analysis

"[D]ream-elements . . . are ungenuine things, substitutes for something else that is unknown to the dreamer . . . the knowledge of which is present in the dreamer but which is inaccessible to him." (113)

"Lusts which we think of as remote from human nature show themselves strong enough to provoke dreams." (143)

"Our dream-interpretations are made on . . . the premises . . . that everything in the mind is determined." (143–144)

"Perhaps there is room in the mind for contrary purposes, for contradictions, to exist side by side." (145)

"The ego, freed from all ethical bonds, also finds itself at one with all the demands of sexual desire, even those which have long been condemned by our aesthetic upbringing and those which contradict all the requirements of moral restraint. The desire for pleasure—the 'libido,' . . . chooses its objects without inhibition, and by preference, indeed, the forbidden ones." (142)

Three Essays on the Theory of Sexuality

"So far as I know, not a single author has clearly recognized the regular existence of a sexual instinct in childhood; and in the writings that have become so numerous on the development of children, the chapter on 'Sexual Development' is as a rule omitted." (173)

"[W]e must assume . . . that the very same impressions that we have forgotten have none the less left the deepest traces on our minds and have had a determining effect upon the whole of our later development." (175)

"Respect for this barrier [incest taboos] is essentially a cultural demand made by society. Society must defend itself against the danger that the interests which it needs for the establishment of higher social units may be swallowed by the family." (225)

"There seems no doubt that germs of sexual impulses are already present in the new-born child and that these continue to develop for a time, but are then overtaken by a progressive period of suppression; this . . . may be held up by individual *peculiarities*." (176)

"Historians of civilization appear to be at one in assuming that powerful components are acquired for every kind of cultural achievement by this diversion of sexual instinctual forces from sexual aims and their direction to new ones— a process which deserves the name of 'sublimation.'" (178)

The Ego and the Id

"The super-ego is, however, not simply a residue of the earliest object-choices of the id; it also represents an energetic reaction-formation against those choices." (34)

The Practice of Psychoanalysis

Notes upon a Case of Obsessional Neurosis

"The unconscious . . . *was* the infantile; it was that part of the self which had become separated off from it in infancy, which had not shared the later stages of its development, and which had in consequence become *repressed*. It was the derivatives of this repressed unconscious that were responsible for the involuntary thoughts which constituted his [the patient's] illness." (315–316)

"[I]t was well known to us that patients derived a certain satisfaction from their sufferings, so that in reality they all resisted their own recovery to some extent." (321)

Implications for Society

The Future of an Illusion

"The principal task of civilization . . . is to defend us against nature." (15)

"[A] man makes the forces of nature . . . into . . . the character of a father. He turns them into gods." (17)

"[I]t became the task of the gods . . . to attend to the sufferings which men inflict on one another." (18)

"Now that God was a single person, man's relations to him could recover the intimacy and intensity of the child's relation to his father. But . . . one wanted to have a reward, or at least to be his only beloved child, his Chosen People. Very much later, pious America laid claim to being 'God's own Country.'" (19)

The Psychogenesis of a Case of Homosexuality in a Woman

"I know, indeed, that the craving of mankind for mysticism is ineradicable, and that it makes ceaseless efforts to win back for mysticism the territory it has been deprived of by *The Interpretation of Dreams.*" (165)

Group Psychology and the Analysis of the Ego

"[E]very religion is . . . a religion of love for all those whom it embraces; while cruelty and intolerance towards those who do not belong to it are natural to every religion." (98)

"[P]sycho-analysis shows that almost every intimate emotional relation between two people which lasts for some time . . . leaves a sediment of feeling of aversion and hostility. . . . The same thing happens when men come together in larger units. . . . The South German cannot endure the North German, the Englishman casts . . . aspersion upon the Scot, the Spaniard despises the Portuguese." (101)

"But when a group is formed the whole of this intolerance vanishes, temporarily or permanently, within the group." (102)

Introductory Lectures on Psycho-Analysis

"[C]onsider the Great War which is . . . laying Europe waste. Think of the vast amount of brutality, cruelty and lies which are able to spread over the civilized world. Do you really believe that a handful of ambitious and deluding men without conscience could have succeeded in unleashing all these evil spirits if their millions of followers did not share their guilt? Do you venture, in such circumstances, to break a lance on behalf of the exclusion of evil from the mental constitution of mankind?" (146)

"We lay a stronger emphasis on what is evil in men only because other people disavow it and thereby make the human mind, not better, but incomprehensible." (147)

Civilization and Its Discontents

"[W]hat decides the purpose of life is simply the programme of the pleasure principle. . . . There is no possibility of its being carried through; all the regulations of the universe run counter to it. One feels inclined to say that the intention that man should be 'happy' is not included in the plan of 'Creation.'" (76)

"What we call happiness . . . comes from the (preferably sudden) satisfaction of needs which have been dammed up to a high degree, and . . . is . . . only possible as an episodic phenomenon." (76)

"[The] replacement of the power of the individual by the power of a community constitutes the decisive step of civilization. The . . . members of the community restrict themselves in their possibilities of satisfaction, whereas the individual knew no such restrictions." (95)

"A good part of the struggles of mankind centre round the single task of finding an expedient accommodation—one . . . that will bring happiness—between this claim [for liberty] of the individual and the cultural claims of the group." (96)

"Civilization has to use its utmost efforts in order to set limits to man's aggressive instincts and to hold the manifestations of them in check by psychical reaction-formations." (112)

"In spite of every effort, these endeavours of civilization have not so far achieved very much." (112)

"The fateful question for the human species seems . . . to be whether . . . their cultural development will succeed in mastering the disturbances of their communal life by the human instinct of aggression and self-destruction." (145)

Notes

Introduction

1. Jared Diamond, "Freud, Influential Yet Unloved." *New York Times*, February 17, 2001.
2. Sigmund Freud, *Introductory Lectures on Psychoanalysis* (New York: Norton, 1966), p. 147.
3. Diamond, "Freud Influential Yet Unloved."
4. This thought is derived from Herbert Marcuse's idea of "repressive de-sublimation." See Herbert Marcuse, *Eros and Civilization* (New York: Vintage Books, 1962), chapter 10.

An Autobiographical Study

1. [Jean Martin Charcot (1825–1893), a French neurologist who experimented with hypnosis in the treatment of nervous diseases. Ed.]
2. ["That shouldn't hinder it from existing." Ed.]
3. [Hysteria is a neurotic disorder exhibiting a variety of symptoms—violent or non-violent emotional outbursts, paralyses, and mental confusion have all been noted. Ed.]
4. [The case being discussed is the now famous "Anna O." Ed.]
5. [Freud's meaning of the term "sexual," especially in regards to children, is often misunderstood. To Freud, early sexual activity is, for example, the child's desire to be held or to enjoy thumb-sucking. Ed.]
6. [Neurasthenia is a mental disorder characterized by fatigue and anxiety. Ed.]
7. [Transference is the defensive and necessary act by the patient of reacting to the therapist as if he or she were a crucially significant other. Ed.]
8. [A "defense" is any verbal or behavioral act which a person employs to avoid the hidden and painful material of his or her neurosis. Ed.]

Introductory Lectures on Psycho-Analysis

1. Frau Dr. von Hug-Hellmuth.
2. [Sacred or holy egotism or selfishness. Ed.]
3. ["That shouldn't hinder it from existing." Ed.]
4. [The reference here is to an edition of the classics prepared by order of Louis XIV for his son which removed material thought to be objectionable. Ed.]

An Outline of Psycho-Analysis

1. Cf. the suggestion that man descended from a mammal which reached sexual maturity at the age of five, but that some major external influence was brought to bear on the species and at that point interrupted the straight course of development of sexuality. Other transformations in the sexual life of man as compared with that of animals might be connected with this—such as the abolition of the periodicity of the libido and the exploitation of the part played by menstruation in the relation between the sexes.

Three Essays on the Theory of Sexuality

1. This weakness would represent the *constitutional* precondition. Psycho-analysis has found that the phenomenon can also be *accidentally* determined, by the occurrence of an early deterrence from sexual activity owing to fear, which may divert the subject from the normal sexual aim and encourage him to seek a substitute for it.

2. Nor is it possible to estimate correctly the part played by heredity until the part played by childhood has been assessed.

3. The assertion made in the text has since struck me myself as being so bold that I have undertaken the task of testing its validity by looking through the literature once more. The outcome of this is that I have allowed my statement to stand unaltered. The scientific examination of both the physical and mental phenomena of sexuality in childhood is still in its earliest beginnings. One writer, Bell (1902, 327), remarks: "I know of no scientist who has given a careful analysis of the emotion as it is seen in the adolescent." Somatic sexual manifestations from the period before puberty have only attracted attention in connection with phenomena of degeneracy and as indications of degeneracy. In none of the accounts which I have read of the psychology of this period of life is a chapter to be found on the erotic life of children; and this applies to the well-known works of Preyer [1882], Baldwin (1898), Pérez (1886), Strümpell (1899), Groos (1904), Heller (1904), Sully (1895) and others. We can obtain the clearest impression of the state of things in this field to-day from the periodical *Die Kinderfehler* from 1896 onwards. Nevertheless the conviction is borne in upon us that the existence of love in childhood stands in no need of discovery. Pérez (1886, 272 ff.) argues in favour of its existence. Groos (1899, 326) mentions as a generally recognized fact that "some children are already accessible to sexual impulses at a very early age and feel an urge to have contact with the opposite sex." The earliest instance of the appearance of "sex-love" recorded by Bell (1902, 330) concerns a child in the middle of his third year. On this point compare further Havelock Ellis (1913, Appendix B).

[*Added* 1910:] This judgement upon the literature of infantile sexuality need no longer be maintained since the appearance of Stanley Hall's exhaustive work (1904). No such modification is necessitated by Moll's recent book (1909). See, on the other hand, Bleuler (1908). [*Added* 1915:] Since this was written, a book by Hug-Hellmuth (1913) has taken the neglected sexual factor fully into account.

4. I have attempted to solve one of the problems connected with the earliest memories of childhood in a paper on "Screen Memories" (1899). [*Added* 1924:] See also Chapter 4 of my *Psychopathology of Everyday Life* (1901).

5. The mechanism of repression cannot be understood unless account is taken of *both* of these two concurrent processes. They may be compared with the manner in which tourists are conducted to the top of the Great Pyramid of Giza by being pushed from one direction and pulled from another.

6. [Sublimation involves the ego redirecting its instinctual energy (libido) to socially acceptable activities, especially those which benefit and strengthen cultural ideals, such as intellectual, scientific, artistic, and humanitarian acts. Ed.]

7. In 1919, a Dr. Galant published, under the title of "Das Lutscherli," the confession of a grown-up girl who had never given up this infantile sexual activity and who represents the satisfaction to be gained from sucking as something completely analogous to sexual satisfaction, particularly when this is obtained from a lover's kiss: "Not every kiss is equal to a 'Lutscherli' [lollipop or popsicle]—no, no, not by any means! It is impossible to describe what a lovely feeling goes through your whole body when you suck; you are right away from this world. You are absolutely satisfied, and happy beyond desire. It is a wonderful feeling; you long for nothing but peace—uninterrupted peace. It is just unspeakably lovely; you feel no pain and no sorrow, and ah! You are carried into another world."

8. Havelock Ellis, it is true, uses the word "auto-erotic" in a somewhat different sense, to describe an excitation which is not provoked from outside but arises internally. What psychoanalysis regards as the essential point is not the genesis of the excitation, but the question of its relation to an object.

9. [Methadone is a drug used to treat heroin addiction. Ed.]

10. [Latency is the fourth stage of psychosexual development. We are, at present, hearing Freud's views on the first (oral) stage. Ed.]

11. Anyone who considers this "sacrilegious" may be recommended to read Havelock Ellis's views [1913, 18] on the relation between mother and child, which agree almost completely with mine.

12. For this explanation of the origin of infantile anxiety I have to thank a three-year-old boy whom I once heard calling out of a dark room: "Auntie, speak to me! I'm frightened because it's so dark." His aunt answered him: "What good would that do? You can't see me." "That doesn't matter," replied the child, "if anyone speaks, it gets light." Thus what he was afraid of was not the dark, but the absence of someone he loved; and he could feel sure of being soothed as soon as he had evidence of that person's presence. [*Added* 1920] One of the most important results of psycho-analytic research is this discovery that neurotic anxiety arises out of libido, that it is the product of a transformation of it, and that it is thus related to it in the same kind of way as vinegar is to wine. A further discussion of this problem will be found in my *Introductory Lectures on Psycho-Analysis* (1916–17), Lecture 225, though even there, it must be confessed, the question is not finally cleared up. [For Freud's latest views on the subject of anxiety, see his *Inhibitions, Symptoms, and Anxiety* (1926) and his *New Introductory Lectures* (1933, chapter 22.]

13. Lou Andreas-Salomé (1916), in a paper which has given us a very much deeper understanding of the significance of anal eroticism, has shown how the history of the first prohibition which a child comes across—the prohibition against getting pleasure from anal activity and its products—has a decisive effect on his whole development. This must be the first occasion on which the infant has a glimpse of an environment hostile to his instinctual impulses, on which he learns to separate his own entity from this alien one and on which he carries out the first "repression" of his possibilities for pleasure. From that time on, what is "anal" remains the symbol of everything that is to be repudiated and excluded from life. The clear-cut distinction between anal and genital processes which is later insisted upon is contradicted by the close anatomical and functional analogies and relation which hold between them. The genital apparatus remains the neighbour of the cloaca, and actually [to quote Lou Andreas-Salomé] "in the case of women is only taken from it on lease."

14. Unusual techniques in carrying out masturbation in later years seem to point to the influence of a prohibition against masturbation which has been overcome.

15. [*Libido* is synonymous with *sexual* and *sexual energy*. Ed.]

16. The barrier against incest is probably among the historical acquisitions of mankind, and, like other moral taboos, has no doubt already become established in many persons by organic inheritance. (Cf. my *Totem and Taboo*, 1912–13.) Psycho-analytic investigation shows, however, how intensely the individual struggles with the temptation to incest during his period of growth and how frequently the barrier is transgressed in phantasies and even in reality.

17. The phantasies of the pubertal period have as their starting-point the infantile sexual researches that were abandoned in childhood. No doubt, too, they are also present before the end of the latency period. They may persist wholly, or to a great extent, unconsciously and for that reason it is often impossible to date them accurately. They are of great importance in the origin of many symptoms, since they precisely constitute preliminary stages of these symptoms and thus lay down the forms in which the repressed libidinal components find satisfaction. In the same way, they are the prototypes of the nocturnal phantasies which become conscious as dreams. Dreams are often nothing more than revivals of pubertal phantasies of this kind under the influence of, and in relation to, some stimulus left over from the waking life of the previous day (the day's residues). [See chapter 7, section 1, of *The Interpretation of Dreams* (1900); standard ed., 5, 492 f.] Some among the sexual phantasies of the pubertal period are especially prominent, and are distinguished by their very general occurrence and by being to a great extent independent of individual experience. Such are the adolescent's phantasies of overhearing his parents in sexual intercourse, of having been seduced at an early age by someone he loves and of having been threatened with castration [cf. the discussion of "primal phantasies" in Lecture 23 of Freud's *Introductory Lectures* (1916–17)]; such, too, are his phantasies of being in the womb, and even of experiences there, and the so-called "Family Romance," in which he reacts to the difference between his attitude towards his parents now and in his childhood. The close relations existing between these phantasies and myths has been demonstrated in the case of the last instance of Otto Rank (1909).

18. We are able to make use of the second of these two sources of material since we are justified in expecting that the early years of children who are later to become neurotic are not likely in this respect to differ *essentially* from those of children who are to grow up into normal adults, [*added* 1915:] but only in the intensity and clarity of the phenomena involved.

Jokes and Their Relation to the Unconscious

1. ["Serenissimus" was the name conventionally given to royal figures by comic magazines during the German Empire. Ed.]

2. ["Zittersprache" refers to stuttering. Ed.]

The Ego and the Id

1. ["Topographical" refers to the division of the psyche into a number of subsystems. Ed.]

2. [Freud is referring to his essay "The Unconscious," which first appeared in two successive issues of the *Zeitschrift* toward the end of 1915. Ed.]

3. Groddeck himself no doubt followed the example of Nietzsche, who habitually used this grammatical term for whatever in our nature is impersonal and, so to speak, subject to natural law.

4. ["Economic" refers to changes in the degrees of sensation linked with internal and external events. Ed.]

5. [Cathexis is the concentration of energy on some object. Identification refers to that object becoming lost or abandoned and appearing in the unconscious mind. Ed.]

6. An interesting parallel to the replacement of object-choice by identification is to be found in the belief of primitive peoples, and in the prohibitions based upon it, that the attributes of animals which are incorporated as nourishment persist as part of the character of those who eat them. As is well known, this belief is one of the roots of cannibalism and its effects have continued through the series of usages of the totem meal down to Holy Communion. The consequences ascribed by this belief to oral mastery of the object do in fact follow in the case of the later sexual object-choice.

7. Perhaps it would be safer to say "with the parents"; for before a child has arrived at definite knowledge of the difference between the sexes, the lack of a penis, it does not distinguish in value between its father and its mother. I recently came across the instance of a young married woman whose story showed that, after noticing the lack of a penis in herself, she had supposed it to be absent not in all women, but only in those whom she regarded as inferior, and had still supposed that her mother possessed one. In order to simplify my presentation I shall discuss only identification with the father.

8. ["Anaclitic" refers to Freud's belief that the instincts for self-preservation (ego-instincts) and the sexual instincts are, at first, attached, but later become independent. The significance of the anaclitic phenomena resides in the belief that the child's caretaker(s) become his or her earliest sexual object(s). Ed.]

9. [This term means "the changes having been made." Ed.]

10. ["Reaction-formation" refers to doing what you would rather not do, but doing it for some benefit (e.g., avoiding another's wrath or staying out of trouble). Ed.]

11. ["Categorical imperative" refers to philosopher Immanuel Kant's notion that a person should only do what he would want another to do. Ed.]

Some Psychical Consequences of the Anatomical Distinction Between the Sexes

1. This is an opportunity for correcting a statement which I made many years ago. I believed that the sexual interest of children, unlike that of pubescents, was aroused, not by the difference between the sexes, but by the problem of where babies come from. We now see that, at all events with girls, this is certainly not the case. With boys it may no doubt happen sometimes one way and sometimes the other; or with both sexes chance experiences may determine the event.

2. In my first critical account of the "History of the Psycho-Analytic Movement" (1914 d), I recognized that this fact represents the core of truth contained in Adler's theory. That theory has no hesitation in explaining the whole world by this single point ("organ-inferiority," the "masculine protest," "breaking away from the feminine line") and prides itself upon having in this way robbed sexuality of its importance and put the desire for power in its place! Thus the only organ which could claim to be called "inferior" without any ambiguity would be the clitoris. On the other hand, one hears of analysts who boast that, though they have worked for dozens of years, they have never found a sign of the existence of the castration complex. We must bow our heads in recognition of the greatness of this achievement, even though it is only a negative one, a piece of virtuosity in the art of over-looking and mistaking. The two theories form an in-

teresting pair of opposites: in the latter not a trace of a castration complex, in the former nothing else than its consequences.

Notes upon a Case of Obsessional Neurosis

1. *Zur Psychopathologie des Alltagslebens,* 1904. [*The Psychopathology of Everyday Life.*]

2. What follows is based upon notes made on the evening of the day of treatment, and adheres as closely as possible to my recollection of the patient's words.— I feel obliged to offer a warning against the practice of noting down what the patient says during the actual time of treatment. The consequent withdrawal of the physician's attention does the patient more harm than can be made up for by any increase in accuracy that may be achieved in the reproduction of his case history.

3. Dr. Alfred Adler, who was formerly an analyst, once drew attention in a privately delivered paper to the peculiar importance which attaches to the *very first* communications made by patients. Here is an instance of this. The patient's opening words laid stress upon the influence exercised over him by men, that is to say, upon the part played in his life by homosexual object-choice; but immediately afterwards they touched upon a second *motif,* which was to become of great importance later on, namely, the conflict between man and woman and the opposition of their interests. Even the fact that he remembered his first pretty governess by her surname, which happened to be a man's Christian name, must be taken into account in this connection. In middle-class circles in Vienna it is more usual to call a governess by her Christian name, and it is by that name that she is more commonly remembered.

4. The patient subsequently admitted that this scene probably occurred one or two years later.

5. "Hofrat" is a title awarded to prominent professionals and civil servants.

6. He said "idea"—the stronger and more significant term "wish," or rather "fear," having evidently been censored. Unfortunately I am not able to reproduce the peculiar indeterminateness of all his remarks.

7. A more detailed description of the event, which the patient gave me later on, made it possible to understand the effect that it produced on him. His uncle, lamenting the loss of his wife, had exclaimed: "Other men allow themselves every possible indulgence, but I lived for this woman alone!" The patient had assumed that his uncle was alluding to his father and was casting doubts upon his conjugal fidelity; and although his uncle had denied this construction of his words most positively, it was no longer possible to counteract their effect.

8. ["Mésalliance" means misalliance; refer to the parenthesis in the same sentence for how the term is used. Ed.]

9. All of this is, of course, only true in the roughest way, but it serves as a first introduction to the subject.

10. Obsessional neurotics are not the only people who are satisfied with euphemisms of this kind.

11. ["Lèse-majesté" refers to a crime against the sovereign power in a state. Ed.]

12. That is, ten years ago.

13. There is here an unmistakable indication of an opposition between the two objects of his love: his father and the "lady."

14. It is never the aim of discussions like this to create conviction. They are only intended to bring the repressed complexes into consciousness, to set the conflict going in the field of con-

scious mental activity, and to facilitate the emergence of fresh material from the unconscious. A sense of conviction is only attained after the patient has himself worked over the reclaimed material, and so long as he is not fully convinced the material must be considered as unexhausted.

15. This sense of guilt involves the most glaring contradiction of his opening denial that he had ever entertained such an evil wish against his father. This is a common type of reaction to repressed material which has become conscious: the "No" with which the fact is first denied is immediately followed by a confirmation of it, though, to begin with, only an indirect one.

16. I only produced these arguments so as once more to demonstrate to myself their inefficacy. I cannot understand how other psychotherapists can assert that they successfully combat neuroses with such weapons as these.

17. It is worth emphasizing that his flight into disease was made possible by his identifying himself with his father. The identification enabled his affects to regress on to the residues of his childhood.

18. Cf. Freud, *Drei Abhandlungen zur Sexualtheorie*, 1905. [*Three Essays on the Theory of Sexuality*.]

19. These alternatives did not exhaust the possibilities. His father had overlooked the commonest outcome of such premature passions—a neurosis.

20. In psycho-analyses we frequently come across occurrences of this kind, dating back to the earliest years of the patient's childhood, in which his infantile sexual activity appears to reach its climax and often comes to a catastrophic end owing to some misfortune or punishment. Such occurrences are apt to appear in a shadowy way in dreams.

21. [The vow referred to involves paying back the charges for his new pince-nez. Keeping his vow, symbolically, keeps the patient obedient to his father—as the cruel captain has become his cruel father and, though mistaken, must be obeyed. By paying the charges, the patient will not be going back to Vienna, and will also see a young lady (not his beloved) and therefore be unfaithful. Ed.]

22. It is perhaps not uninteresting to observe that once again obedience to his father coincided with abandoning the lady. If he had stopped and paid back the money to A., he would have made atonement to his father, and at the same time he would have deserted his lady in favour of some one else more attractive. In this conflict the lady had been victorious—with the assistance, to be sure, of the patient's own normal good sense.

The Psychogenesis of a Case of Homosexuality in a Woman

1. [*Sine qua non* refers to something which is essential. Ed.]

2. It is by no means rare for a love-relation to be broken off through a process of identification on the part of the lover with the loved object, a process equivalent to a kind of regression to narcissism. After this has been accomplished, it is easy in making a fresh choice of object to direct the libido to a member of the sex opposite to that of the earlier choice.

3. The displacements of the libido here described are doubtless familiar to every analyst from investigation of the anamneses of neurotics. With the latter, however, they occur in early childhood, at the time of the early efflorescence of erotic life; with our patient, who was in no way neurotic, they took place in the first years following puberty, though, incidentally, they were just as completely unconscious. Perhaps one day this temporal factor may turn out to be of great importance.

4. As "retiring in favour of someone else" has not previously been mentioned among the causes of homosexuality, or in the mechanism of libidinal fixation in general, I will adduce here another analytic observation of the same kind which has a special feature of interest. I once knew two twin brothers, both of whom were endowed with strong libidinal impulses. One of them was very successful with women, and had innumerable affairs with women and girls. The other went the same way at first, but it became unpleasant for him to be trespassing on his brother's preserves, and, owing to the likeness between them, to be mistaken for him on intimate occasions; so he got out of the difficulty by becoming homosexual. He left the women to his brother, and thus retired in his favour. Another time I treated a youngish man, an artist, unmistakably bisexual in disposition, in whom the homosexual trend had come to the fore simultaneously with a disturbance in his work. He fled from both women and work together. The analysis, which was able to bring him back to both, showed that fear of his father was the most powerful psychical motive for both the disturbances, which were really renunciations. In his imagination all women belonged to his father, and he sought refuge in men out of submission, so as to retire from the conflict with his father. Such a motivation of the homosexual object-choice must be by no means uncommon; in the primaeval ages of the human race all women presumably belonged to the father and head of the primal horde.

Among brothers and sisters who are not twins this "retiring" plays a great part in other spheres as well as in that of erotic choice. For example, an elder brother studies music and is admired for it; the younger, far more gifted musically, soon gives up his own musical studies, in spite of his fondness for it, and cannot be persuaded to touch an instrument again. This is only one example of a very frequent occurrence, and investigation of the motives leading to this "retirement" rather than to open rivalry discloses very complicated conditions in the mind.

5. [A "talion" is a punishment that fits the crime; Freud is referring, in other words, to the same principle as "an eye for an eye." Ed.]

Female Sexuality

1. It is to be anticipated that male analysts with feminist sympathies, and our women analysts also, will disagree with what I have said here. They will hardly fail to object that such notions have their origin in the man's "masculinity complex," and are meant to justify theoretically his innate propensity to disparage and suppress women. But this sort of psycho-analytic argument reminds us here, as it so often does, of Dostoevsky's famous "knife that cuts both ways." The opponents of those who reason thus will for their part think it quite comprehensible that members of the female sex should refuse to accept a notion that appears to gainsay their eagerly coveted equality with men. The use of analysis as a weapon of controversy obviously leads to no decision.

Totem and Taboo

1. "The Totem bond is stronger than the bond of blood or family in the modern sense." (Frazer, 1919, 1, 53.)

2. This highly condensed summary of the totemic system must necessarily be subject to further comments and qualifications. The word "totem" was first introduced in 1791 (in the form "totam") from the North American Indians by an Englishman, J. Long. The subject itself has gradually attracted great scientific interest and has produced a copious literature, from which

I may select as works of capital importance J. G. Frazer's four-volume *Totemism and Exogamy* (1910) and the writings of Andrew Lang, e.g. *The Secret of the Totem* (1905). The merit of having been the first to recognize the importance of totemism for human prehistory lies with a Scotsman, John Ferguson McLennan (1869–70). Totemic institutions were, or still are, to be observed in operation, not only among the Australians, but also among the North American Indians, among the peoples of Oceania, in the East Indies and in a large part of Africa. It may also be inferred from certain vestigial remains, for which it is otherwise hard to account, that totemism existed at one time among the Aryan and Semitic aboriginal races of Europe and Asia. Many investigators are therefore inclined to regard it as a necessary phase of human development which has been passed through universally.

How did prehistoric men come to adopt totems? How, that is, did they come to make the fact of their being descended from one animal or another the basis of their social obligations and, as we shall see presently, of their sexual restrictions? There are numerous theories on the subject—of which Wundt (1906 [264 ff.]) has given an epitome for German readers—but no agreement. It is my intention to devote a special study before long to the problem of totemism, in which I shall attempt to solve it by the help of a psycho-analytic line of approach. (See the fourth essay in this work.)

Not only, however, is the *theory* of totemism a matter of dispute; the facts themselves are scarcely capable of being expressed in general terms as I have tried to do in the text above. There is scarcely a statement which does not call for exceptions and contradictions. But it must not be forgotten that even the most primitive and conservative races are in some sense *ancient* races and have a long past history behind them during which their original conditions of life have been subject to much development and distortion. So it comes about that in those races in which totemism exists to-day, we may find it in various stages of decay and disintegration or in the process of transition to other social and religious institutions, or again in a stationary condition which may differ greatly from the original one. The difficulty in this last case is to decide whether we should regard the present state of things as a true picture of the significant features of the past or as a secondary distortion of them.

3. On the other hand, at all events so far as this prohibition is concerned, the father, who is a Kangaroo, is free to commit incest with his daughters, who are Emus. If the totem descended through the *male* line, however, the Kangaroo father would be prohibited from incest with his daughters (since all his children would be Kangaroos), whereas the son would be free to commit incest with his mother. These implications of totem prohibitions suggest that descent through the female line is older than that through the male, since there are grounds for thinking that totem prohibitions were principally directed against the incestuous desires of the son.

4. [Darwin theorized that, similar to the higher apes, primitive men lived in small groups, or "primal hordes," where the oldest and strongest's jealousy kept the others from his many wives. Ed.]

5. To avoid possible misunderstanding, I must ask the reader to take into account the final sentences of the following footnote as a corrective to this description.

6. This hypothesis, which has such a monstrous air, of the tyrannical father being overwhelmed and killed by a combination of his exiled sons, was also arrived at by Atkinson (1903, 220 f.) as a direct implication of the state of affairs in Darwin's primal horde: "The patriarch had only one enemy whom he should dread . . . a youthful band of brothers living together in forced celibacy, or at most in polyandrous relation with some single female captive. A horde as yet weak in their impubescence they are, but they would, when strength was gained with time, in-

evitably wrench by combined attacks, renewed again and again, both wife and life from the paternal tyrant." Atkinson, who incidentally passed his whole life in New Caledonia and had unusual opportunities for studying the natives, also pointed out that the conditions which Darwin assumed to prevail in the primal horde may easily be observed in herds of wild oxen and horses and regularly lead to the killing of the father of the herd. [Ibid., 222 f.] He further supposed that, after the father had been disposed of, the horde would be disintegrated by a bitter struggle between the victorious sons. Thus any new organization of society would be precluded: there would be "an ever-recurring violent succession to the solitary paternal tyrant, by sons whose parricidal hands were so soon again clenched in fraternal strife." [Ibid., 228.] Atkinson, who had no psycho-analytic hints to help him and who was ignorant of Robertson Smith's studies, found a less violent transition from the primal horde to the next social stage, at which numbers of males live together in a peaceable community. He believed that through the intervention of maternal love the sons—to begin with only the youngest, but later others as well—were allowed to remain with the horde, and that in return for this toleration the sons acknowledged their father's sexual privilege by renouncing all claim to their mother and sisters. [Ibid., 231 ff.]

Such is the highly remarkable theory put forward by Atkinson. In its essential feature it is in agreement with my own; but its divergence results in its failing to effect a correlation with many other issues.

The lack of precision in what I have written in the text above, its abbreviation of the time factor and its compression of the whole subject matter, may be attributed to the reserve necessitated by the nature of the topic. It would be as foolish to aim at exactitude in such questions as it would be unfair to insist upon certainty.

7. This fresh emotional attitude must also have been assisted by the fact that the deed cannot have given complete satisfaction to those who did it. From one point of view it had been done in vain. Not one of the sons had in fact been able to put his original wish—of taking his father's place—into effect. And, as we know, failure is far more propitious for a moral reaction than satisfaction.

8. "Murder and incest, or offences of a like kind against the sacred laws of blood, are in primitive society the only crimes of which the community as such takes cognizance." (Smith, 1894, 419.)

9. "To us moderns, for whom the breach which divides the human and the divine has deepened into an impassable gulf, such mimicry may appear impious, but it was otherwise with the ancients. To their thinking gods and men were akin, for many families traced their descent from a divinity, and the deification of a man probably seemed as little extraordinary to them as the canonization of a saint seems to a modern Catholic." (Frazer, 1911a, 2, 177 f.)

10. It is generally agreed that when, in mythologies, one generation of gods is overcome by another, what is denoted is the historical replacement of one religious system by a new one, whether as a result of foreign conquest or of psychological development. In the latter case myth approximates to what Silberer [1909] has described as "functional phenomena."

11. Fear of castration plays an extremely large part, in the case of the youthful neurotics whom we come across, as an interference in their relations with their father. The illuminating instance reported by Fereczi (1913) has shown us how a little boy took as his totem the beast that had pecked at his little penis. When our [Jewish] children come to hear of ritual circumcision, they equate it with castration. The parallel in social psychology to this reaction by children has not yet been worked out, so far as I am aware. In primaeval times and in primitive races,

where circumcision is so frequent, it is performed at the age of initiation into manhood and it is at that age that its significance is to be found; it was only as a secondary development that it was shifted back to the early years of life. It is of very great interest to find that among primitive peoples circumcision is combined with cutting the hair and knocking out teeth or is replaced by them, and that our children, who cannot possibly have any knowledge of this, in fact treat these two operations, in the anxiety with which they react to them, as equivalents of castration.

12. We find that impulses to suicide in a neurotic turn out regularly to be self-punishments for wishes for someone else's death.

13. Frazer (1912, 2, 51). No one familiar with the literature of the subject will imagine that the derivation of Christian communion from the totem meal is an idea originating from the author of the present essay.

Group Psychology and the Analysis of the Ego

1. ["Eros" connotes the "life instincts," understood as those instincts which seek to preserve existence. Ed.]

2. ["ihnen zu Liebe" means "for love of them." Ed.]

3. In groups, the attributes "stable" and "artificial" seem to coincide or at least to be intimately connected.

4. ["Economically" refers to the quantity of psychic energy (libido) employed upon an object. Ed.]

5. "A company of porcupines crowded themselves very close together one cold winter's day so as to profit by one another's warmth and so save themselves from being frozen to death. But soon they felt one another's quills, which induced them to separate again. And now, when the need for warmth brought them nearer together again, the second evil arose once more. So that they were driven backwards and forwards from one trouble to the other, until they had discovered a mean distance at which they could most tolerably exist." (*Parerga und Paralipomena*, Part 2, 31, "Gleichnisse und Parabelm.")

6. Perhaps with the solitary exception of the relation of a mother to her son, which is based on narcissism, is not disturbed by subsequent rivalry, and is reinforced by a rudimentary attempt at object-choice.

7. In a recently published study, *Beyond the Pleasure Principle,* I have attempted to connect the polarity of love and hatred with a hypothetical opposition between instincts of life and death, and to establish the sexual instincts as the purest examples of the former, the instincts of life.

Civilization and Its Discontents

1. Goethe, indeed, warns us that "nothing is harder to bear than a succession of fair days." But this may be an exaggeration.

2. [Freud is referring to his earlier statement: "We are threatened with suffering from three directions: from our own body, which is doomed to decay and dissolution and which cannot even do without pain and anxiety as warning signals; from the external world, which may rage against us with overwhelming and merciless forces of destruction; and finally from our relations to other men." Ed.]

3. Anyone who has tasted the miseries of poverty in his own youth, and has experienced the indifference and arrogance of the well-to-do, should be safe from the suspicion of having no understanding or good will towards endeavours to fight against the inequality of wealth among men and all that it leads to. To be sure, if an attempt is made to base this fight upon an abstract demand, in the name of justice, for equality for all men, there is a very obvious objection to be made—that nature, by endowing individuals with extremely unequal attributes and mental capacities, has introduced injustices against which there is no remedy.